The One-Dish Vegetarian

The
One-Dish
Vegetarian

Maria Robbins

St. Martin's Press ❧ New York

For Ken

THE ONE-DISH VEGETARIAN.

The following recipes originally appeared in the author's book *Chili!*:
Andy Weil's Vegetarian Chili, Bean and Corn Chili, Black Bean Confetti
Chili, Chili con Tempeh, Sag Harbor's Vegetarian Chili, and Green Chili
with White Beans.

ISBN 0-312-18151-5

Designed by Richard Oriolo

Interior Illustrations © 1998 by Lauren Jarrett

First Edition: September 1998

10 9 8 7 6 5 4 3 2 1

Contents

The One-Dish Vegetarian

Introduction

I should own up at the outset to the fact that I am not a full-time vegetarian. My husband and I eat red meat occasionally, and chicken and fish more frequently. I do try to buy chicken and meat that have been fed vegetarian diets with no added hormones or antibiotics. But for reasons of health, weight control, and general well-being, we have become, like more and more people, part-time vegetarians. The transition, whether in full or half measures, does not come easily.

As with most people who grew up with or were influenced by Anglo-European traditions, dinner didn't look like dinner to us unless it was built around a roast or a joint of meat for a "main course"—a chunk of protein anchoring the menu, with vegetables and grains in supporting roles, or even only in decorative ones. When one tries to think about creating a vegetarian meal, trust me, this model is not much help.

Even for the most accomplished cook, planning meals suddenly becomes complicated and confusing. If the main course is veggies, what side dishes do you serve? How many side dishes should there be, and how do you make them look (and taste) different? Eventually, a simple roast and two veg start to look awfully good again.

It was from these kinds of considerations that I started to think about simplifying my approach by devising and collecting one-dish vegetarian meals. Any accompaniments were simple basics, like good bread and a green salad. There were other considerations to take into account. Neither my husband nor I enjoy tofu, tempeh, seitan, or any of the meat replacements that are commonly found in health food stores or some vegetarian restaurants. But we do enjoy pasta, grains, and a wide variety of vegetables and beans. We like spicy foods, curries, chili, and robust soups and stews. Clearly there was a lot to work with.

I decided to begin with dishes we already knew and loved. I noticed that when I served pasta dishes such as Spaghetti with Caramelized Onions, Linguine with Spring Vegetables, Buckwheat Pasta with Cabbage and Sage, or Farfalle with Mushrooms, no one ever noticed that the meal was vegetarian. They were too busy eating to think about what wasn't there.

The same proved true of risotto. A steaming bowl of Risotto with Butternut Squash, or Risotto with Eggplant and Tomato, is so hearty and satisfying that nothing other than a green salad is wanted. Soups make fabulous one-dish vegetarian meals, and while some of them take a little time to prepare they are all as good or better on the days after. I turned to cuisines from Asia and India for curries, stews, and noodle and fried-rice dishes. I cooked for family and friends, and everybody loved the hearty simplicity of a meal in a bowl. I never talked about what the food didn't have and no one much noticed that they were eating vegetarian.

I now cook vegetarian as often as not. I like the way I feel when I eat these satisfying but lighter dishes, but mostly I love the vibrant tastes and flavors of vegetable-based dishes. And because too often life becomes very complicated, I love the simplicity of a one-dish meal.

Salads

Barley-Corn Salad from Santa Fe

6 main-course servings with leftovers

Two summers ago, I spent a month in Santa Fe, visiting friends who were happy to let me use their kitchen to cook with baskets of produce I picked up from the amazing farmer's market nearby. I went to the farmer's market as often as I could, and one day I noticed that Deborah Madison, one of my favorite cookbook writers, was giving a talk. This was a treat—and from her talk that day I learned the combination of fresh herbs that I've used in this salad.

3 cups cooked and cooled pearl barley (see page 162)

2 cups cooked, fresh or frozen corn kernels

2 cups cooked black beans (drain and rinse them if canned)

4 medium-size ripe tomatoes, chopped

3 serrano or jalapeño peppers, ribbed, seeded, and chopped

1 small red onion, finely chopped

1 cup diced jicama

2 tablespoons finely chopped fresh cilantro

2 tablespoons finely chopped fresh parsley

2 tablespoons finely chopped fresh basil

2 tablespoons finely chopped fresh dill

1 garlic clove

$\frac{1}{2}$ teaspoon salt

$\frac{1}{2}$ teaspoon toasted cumin (see page 172)

$\frac{1}{4}$ cup fresh lime juice

1 tablespoon rice vinegar

1 tablespoon white wine, broth, or orange juice

1 teaspoon sugar

$\frac{1}{4}$ cup extra-virgin olive oil

1. In a large bowl, combine barley, corn, black beans, tomatoes, serrano or jalapeño pepper, onion, jicama, and the herbs.

2. In a mortar, crush the garlic clove together with the salt and cumin. Mash them to a paste. Whisk in lime juice, vinegar, wine, and sugar. Whisk until the sugar dissolves, then whisk in olive oil.

3. Pour over the salad and toss to mix. Taste for seasoning and add additional salt and freshly ground black pepper to taste. This salad can sit covered and at room temperature for several hours before serving. It can be made a day ahead, covered, re-frigerated, and returned to room temperature before serving.

The near end of the street was rather dark and had mostly vegetable shops. Abundance of vegetables—piles of white and green fennel, like celery, and great sheaves of young, purplish, sea-dust—coloured artichokes, nodding their buds, piles of great radishes, scarlet and bluey purple, carrots, long strings of dried figs, mountains of big oranges, scarlet large peppers, a large slice of pumpkin, a great mass of colours and vegetable freshnesses . . . —D.H. Lawrence, *Sea and Sardinia*

Quinoa Salad with Apples, Pears, Fennel, and Walnuts

This is a pretty and delicious salad to serve for a special lunch or as part of a buffet with other vegetarian dishes.

3 cups cooked quinoa (see page 163)

2 apples, peeled, cored, diced, and sprinkled with lemon juice

2 ripe pears, peeled, cored, diced, and sprinkled with lemon juice

1 small fennel bulb, trimmed and diced

$\frac{1}{2}$ cup dried currants

2 shallots, finely minced

$\frac{1}{2}$ cup fresh orange juice

3 tablespoons fresh lemon juice

1 tablespoon extra-virgin olive oil

Freshly grated rind of 1 orange

Freshly grated rind of 1 lemon

Salt, to taste

Freshly ground black pepper, to taste

$\frac{1}{2}$ cup chopped, toasted walnuts

1. In a large bowl, combine the quinoa, apples, pears, fennel, currants, and shallots.

2. In a small bowl, whisk together the orange juice, lemon juice, olive oil, orange and lemon rinds, salt, and pepper. Pour over the quinoa salad and mix well. Sprinkle with walnuts and serve.

Quinoa Potato Salad

4 to 6 main-course servings

This recipe is adapted from one in The Splendid Grain *by Rebecca Wood, which is a wonderful book, full of serious information and inspired ideas for cooking with most of the grains available to us today. Rebecca Wood, in turn, credits her recipe to Gisela Weischede, the sub-abbess of the Crestone Mountain Zen Monastery in Colorado. I changed the dressing to a lighter one using vinegar, wine, and miso. This salad is utterly delicious and satisfying.*

$1\frac{1}{2}$ to 2 pounds fingerling, Yukon Gold, or red potatoes, well scrubbed

$\frac{1}{4}$ cup seasoned rice vinegar or apple cider vinegar plus $\frac{1}{2}$ teaspoon sugar

$\frac{1}{4}$ cup white wine

1 tablespoon extra-virgin olive oil

2 tablespoons white miso

1 tablespoon Dijon mustard

$\frac{1}{2}$ cup finely chopped shallots

2 cups cooked quinoa (see page 163)

$\frac{3}{4}$ cup chopped dill pickles

2 celery ribs, finely diced

$\frac{1}{4}$ cup finely minced fresh parsley

$\frac{1}{4}$ cup finely minced fresh dill

Salt, to taste

Freshly ground black pepper, to taste

1. Put the potatoes in a saucepan with enough water to cover. Bring to a boil over high heat and cook for 20 minutes. Pierce a potato with a knife to see if they are done. They should be cooked through but still firm. Cook for another 5 to 10 minutes if necessary and drain the potatoes in a colander. Let the potatoes cool until you can handle them, but they should still be warm. Warm potatoes will absorb more of the dressing. Leave the potato skins on or remove them as you wish.

2. While the potatoes are cooking, whisk together the vinegar, white wine, olive oil, miso, and Dijon mustard in a large bowl. Stir in the shallots and set aside.

3. Slice fingerling potatoes into $\frac{1}{4}$-inch-thick rounds, or dice the potatoes into $\frac{1}{2}$-inch cubes. Add the potatoes to the dressing and toss well. Add the quinoa, pickles, celery, parsley, and dill. Toss well to combine, taste, and add salt and freshly ground pepper as needed. This salad tastes best if served lukewarm or at room temperature. It will lose some flavor if it is refrigerated.

Lentil Salad

4 to 6 main-dish servings

 Serve this yummy salad surrounded by Belgian endive leaves or mounted on a bed of greens.

2 cups green lentils (lentilles du Puy) or brown lentils
$\frac{1}{4}$ cup Balsamic Vinaigrette (see page 166)
2 ripe tomatoes, cut into small dice
1 carrot, cut into small dice
1 small celery rib, cut into small dice
3 scallions, white and some green parts, sliced into thin rounds
Salt, to taste
Freshly ground black pepper, to taste

1. Put the lentils in a medium-size saucepan and cover with 6 cups cold water. Bring the water to a boil, reduce to a simmer, and cook, uncovered, for 15 to 20 minutes, until lentils are cooked but still a little chewy.

2. Drain the lentils and place them in a bowl. Add the Balsamic Vinaigrette while the lentils are warm and mix well.

3. Add the diced tomatoes, carrot, celery, and scallions. Mix well and season with salt and pepper to taste. Serve the salad warm, at room temperature, or cold. The salad will keep quite well, tightly covered, in the refrigerator for 2 days.

Oat Salad with Summer Vegetables

I love oats in almost any form. Without oatmeal, my breakfasts would be truly bereft. But whole oats, also called oat groats, can be enjoyed for lunch and dinner as well. One of my favorites is this salad which makes a very satisfying nutrition-packed one-dish meal.

1 cup whole oats (oat groats)

$1\frac{3}{4}$ cups water

$\frac{1}{2}$ teaspoon salt

1 tablespoon unsalted butter or sesame oil (optional)

$\frac{1}{2}$ cup finely minced shallots

$\frac{1}{2}$ cup finely chopped fresh parsley

$\frac{1}{4}$ cup shredded basil leaves

1 pint vine-ripened cherry tomatoes, quartered

4 small kirby cucumbers, scrubbed clean and diced

1 red bell pepper, diced

2 tablespoons extra-virgin olive oil

2 tablespoons fresh lemon juice

Salt, to taste

Freshly ground black pepper, to taste

Gomasio (see page 169)

1. Toast the oats in a cast iron skillet or wok over high heat, stirring constantly, for about 4 minutes. The oats should be aromatic and just start to take on color.

2. Bring the water, salt, and butter or oil to a boil over high heat. Add the oats, lower the heat, and simmer, covered, for 45 minutes, until liquid is absorbed and the oats are tender. Remove pan from heat and let stand, covered, for 10 minutes.

3. While the oats are cooking, combine the shallots, parsley, basil, tomatoes, cucumbers, and red pepper in a large bowl.

4. In a small bowl, whisk together the olive oil and lemon juice.

5. Fluff the oats with a fork and add them to the vegetables in the bowl. Toss together, add the olive oil mixture, and toss again. Season with salt and pepper to taste and serve warm or at room temperature. Pass a small bowl of Gomasio for garnish.

Summer Bulgur Salad with Fruit

4 to 6 main-course servings

Here is another fruit-and-grain salad that you and your guests will love. You can vary the fruit according to what is fresh and ripe at the market. Consider apricots, peaches, plums, grapes, pineapple, or papaya. In the fall and winter, switch to apples, pears, and orange sections.

6 cups water
2 cups bulgur
2 cups diced ripe mango
2 cups diced ripe nectarines
4 scallions, trimmed and sliced into very thin rounds
2 fresh serrano or jalapeño chilies, stemmed, seeded, and finely minced
$\frac{1}{3}$ cup fresh mint leaves snipped into fine ribbons with scissors
$\frac{1}{4}$ cup fresh lime juice
$\frac{1}{4}$ cup extra-virgin olive oil
Salt, to taste
Freshly ground black pepper, to taste

1. In a saucepan, bring the water to a boil. Turn off the heat, stir in the bulgur, cover, and let stand for 30 minutes. Drain the bulgur in a fine-mesh sieve. Spread it out on a clean kitchen towel, roll up the long sides like a jelly roll, then twist the ends to squeeze out as much of the remaining moisture as possible.

2. Place the bulgur in a large bowl. Add the mango, nectarines, scallions, chilies, and snipped mint leaves. In a small bowl, whisk together the lime juice and olive oil and pour over the salad. Toss the salad well to combine all the ingredients. Season with salt and pepper to taste. Serve the salad at room temperature or refrigerator cold.

Variations

- Add $\frac{1}{2}$ cup chopped, toasted walnuts.
- Add $\frac{1}{2}$ cup crumbled feta cheese.
- Add $\frac{1}{2}$ cup currants or raisins.
- Substitute other fresh herbs for the mint. Consider lemon balm, basil, dill, lemon thyme, and parsley.

Black Bean Confetti Salad

4 to 6 main-dish servings

If you haven't had time to cook the black beans yourself, you can substitute with great success canned beans that have been rinsed and drained. This way you can have a main-course salad prepared in minutes. Serve this colorful salad with corn bread or tortilla chips.

4 cups cooked black beans (see page 168)

2 cups cooked corn kernels

1 large red or Vidalia onion, cut into $\frac{1}{4}$-inch dice

3 large carrots, cut into fine dice

1 large red bell pepper, seeded and cut into $\frac{1}{4}$-inch dice

2 hot fresh chili peppers, seeded and finely chopped

1 cup finely minced fresh cilantro

2 large garlic cloves

1 teaspoon coarse salt

$\frac{1}{2}$ teaspoon whole, toasted cumin seeds

2 tablespoons balsamic vinegar

2 tablespoons fresh lime juice, plus additional, to taste

2 tablespoons extra-virgin olive oil

Freshly ground black pepper, to taste

1. In a large bowl, combine the beans, corn kernels, onion, carrots, bell pepper, chili peppers, and fresh cilantro.

2. In a mortar and pestle, mash the garlic, salt, and cumin seeds to a paste. Stir in the vinegar and lime juice and mix to dissolve the salt. Whisk in the olive oil. Pour over the bean salad and mix well. Taste for seasoning and add freshly ground black pepper and more lime juice to taste.

Variations

- Add 2 or 3 chopped, very ripe tomatoes to the salad.
- Add about 1½ cups finely diced jicama.
- Add 1 large, medium-ripe mango, peeled, pitted, and chopped.
- For added heat and a great smoky flavor, add 1 chipotle chile in adobo sauce to the mashed garlic and salt.

No one has yet found a way, luckily, to botch the lowly bean the way wheat flour and white rice have been ruined. If a person is still interested in a food that is cheap, keeps indefinitely while in the dry state, is low in fat, high in protein, and improves in flavor each time it is reheated, he'll do well to stock up on sacks of pinto beans.
—Stella Hughes, *Bacon & Beans, Ranch-Country Recipes*

Wild Rice Waldorf Salad

The addition of wild rice to the ingredients of a Waldorf salad transforms it into a hearty one-dish meal. Serve for lunch or dinner with a leaf lettuce salad on the side.

4 cups steamed and cooled wild rice (see page 162)

2 large apples, peeled, cored, and diced

2 celery ribs, halved lengthwise and thinly sliced

2 carrots, cut into fine dice

1 cup halved seedless grapes

¾ cup chopped, toasted walnuts

½ cup raisins or currants

½ cup soy mayonnaise or reduced-fat mayonnaise

2 to 3 tablespoons fresh lemon juice

Salt, to taste

Freshly ground black pepper, to taste

1. In a large bowl, combine the rice, apples, celery, carrots, grapes, walnuts, and raisins or currants.

2. In a small bowl, blend the mayonnaise with 2 tablespoons lemon juice. Add to the salad ingredients, mix well, and taste for seasoning. Add more lemon juice if you like, and salt and pepper to taste.

Variations

- Any combination of grains work well in this salad. If you have any leftover white or brown rice (see pages 160 or 161), cooked barley (see page 162), bulgur, or wheat berries, you can substitute that for any part of the wild rice.
- If you dislike mayonnaise, use any vinaigrette instead.

Couscous Salad

A lovely salad to serve for dinner alongside a fresh green salad. Cook the couscous while you prepare the other ingredients. The salad will easily be done in twenty minutes.

3 tablespoons extra-virgin olive oil

2 garlic cloves, finely minced

$\frac{3}{4}$ teaspoon cinnamon

$\frac{1}{2}$ teaspoon ground ginger

$\frac{1}{2}$ teaspoon ground cumin (see page 172)

$\frac{1}{4}$ teaspoon turmeric

2 cups vegetable stock

1 cup couscous (see page 163)

1 large carrot, shredded

1 small red bell pepper, cut into $\frac{1}{4}$-inch dice

1 small zucchini, cut into $\frac{1}{4}$-inch dice

1 small red onion, cut into $\frac{1}{4}$-inch dice

1 large, tart apple, peeled, cored and cut into $\frac{1}{4}$-inch dice

$\frac{1}{3}$ cup golden raisins

2 cups canned chick-peas, rinsed and drained

$\frac{1}{4}$ cup finely minced fresh parsley

$\frac{1}{4}$ cup fresh lemon juice

1 teaspoon salt

Freshly ground black pepper, to taste

1. Heat 2 tablespoons olive oil in a 2-quart saucepan over medium heat. Add the garlic, cinnamon, ginger, cumin, and turmeric. Cook, stirring, for 30 seconds. Add the vegetable stock and bring to a simmer.

2. Stir in the couscous in a steady stream and bring to a boil, stirring constantly. Remove from the heat, cover, and let stand for 15 minutes.

3. Transfer the couscous to a large bowl, fluff with a fork, and let cool until tepid.

4. Add the carrot, bell pepper, zucchini, onion, apple, raisins, chick-peas, and parsley, and mix well. In a small bowl, whisk together the remaining tablespoon of olive oil, lemon juice, salt, and freshly ground black pepper. Pour over salad ingredients and mix well.

5. Serve at room temperature or chilled. The salad will keep, covered in the refrigerator for several days.

Potato Salad with Green Beans and Tomatoes

4 to 6 main-dish servings

This is my version of a potato and green bean salad that I learned to make in my work with Ruth von Waerebeek on our cookbook, Everybody Eats Well in Belgium. *It is a salad most closely associated with the city of Liège, the birthplace of Georges Simenon, the creator of the world-famous Inspector Maigret mysteries.*

$\frac{1}{4}$ cup good white wine

$\frac{1}{4}$ cup white wine vinegar

1 teaspoon salt

1 teaspoon sugar

Freshly ground black pepper

2 tablespoons extra-virgin olive oil

$\frac{1}{2}$ cup finely minced shallots

$1\frac{1}{2}$ pounds thin-skinned new potatoes

1 pound green beans, trimmed and snapped in half

$\frac{1}{2}$ teaspoon salt

4 to 6 fresh, ripe tomatoes

Salt, to taste
$\frac{1}{4}$ cup finely minced fresh parsley
2 tablespoons finely minced fresh dill

1. In a large bowl, whisk together the white wine, wine vinegar, salt, sugar, and freshly ground black pepper, until both salt and sugar are dissolved. Whisk in the olive oil and shallots, and set aside.

2. Place the potatoes in a medium-size pot, add water to cover, and bring to a boil. Cook, uncovered, for 20 minutes, until the potatoes are fork tender. Drain the potatoes in a colander and let them cool until you can handle them. While the potatoes are still warm, peel and cut them into $\frac{1}{4}$-inch-thick slices. Place warm potato slices in the salad bowl with the vinaigrette. Mix well.

3. Bring a large pot of water a boil and add the green beans and salt. Cook, uncovered, for 5 minutes, until the beans are cooked but still crunchy. Drain the beans in a colander and add them to the potatoes in the bowl. Mix well.

4. Core the tomatoes and slice them into $\frac{1}{2}$-inch-thick rounds. Arrange the rounds on plates and season with salt and freshly ground black pepper.

5. Season the potato salad to taste with additional salt and freshly ground black pepper. Add the parsley and dill, and spoon the salad onto the tomato rounds. Serve while the salad is still slightly warm.

Variations

- Instead of fresh dill you can substitute any of the following fresh herbs: 1 tablespoon finely minced fresh tarragon; or 1 tablespoon fresh thyme leaves; or 1 tablespoon fresh chervil leaves. Don't substitute dried herbs; if you don't have fresh, leave them out.
- Add 2 or 3 chopped, ripe tomatoes to the dressed salad.
- Add 1 cup cooked corn kernels to the dressed salad.

Brown Rice and Lentil Salad

This is a hearty main-course salad that is filling, satisfying, and delicious. It makes a perfect brown-bag lunch, as it tastes best at room temperature. Pack it into a small plastic container and take it with you to work or on a long hike. With a piece of fruit, you won't need another thing.

1 cup brown lentils, picked over and rinsed

3 cups water

1 teaspoon salt

$\frac{1}{4}$ cup extra-virgin olive oil

3 cups cooked brown rice (see page 161)

1 red bell pepper, seeded and cut into small dice

1 green bell pepper, seeded and cut into small dice

1 medium red onion, cut into small dice

1 bunch scallions, trimmed and thinly sliced

2 celery ribs, cut into small dice

1 large carrot, cut into small dice

$\frac{1}{2}$ cup finely chopped parsley

1 garlic clove

$\frac{1}{2}$ teaspoon salt

$\frac{1}{2}$ cup rice vinegar

Freshly ground black pepper, to taste

1. Combine the lentils, water, and salt in a saucepan and cook the lentils over moderately high heat for 10 to 15 minutes, until they are al dente. Drain the lentils, reserving the cooking water, and place them in a large salad bowl. Drizzle the lentils with 2 tablespoons of olive oil, add the rice, and toss to combine.

2. Add the peppers, onion, scallions, celery, carrot, and parsley to lentils and rice and toss to combine.

3. In a mortar, crush the garlic together with the salt. Add the vinegar and mix. Stir in the remaining olive oil. Pour the dressing over the salad and toss to combine. Season to taste with additional salt, if necessary, and freshly ground black pepper.

I . . . consider the eating of lentils promotes an even temper. Even temper and satiated appetite—need we ask for anything more?
—Pliny

Wild Rice and Corn Salad

You can prepare this salad hours ahead of time. Just keep it covered, at room temperature, until serving time.

1 cup wild rice (see page 162)

3 cups water

1 teaspoon salt

2 tablespoons extra-virgin olive oil

3 tablespoons balsamic vinegar

$\frac{1}{2}$ teaspoon salt

Freshly ground black pepper, to taste

2 large ripe tomatoes, coarsely chopped

3 scallions, trimmed and thinly sliced

1 cup cooked corn kernels, cut from 2 ears of corn

$\frac{1}{4}$ cup slivered almonds, toasted

Washed salad greens

1. Put the rice in a large bowl of cold water and scrub the grains between the palms of your hands. Drain the rice in a strainer. Bring the water and salt to a boil. Add the wild rice, reduce heat, and simmer, partially covered, until tender. This will take anywhere from 40 to 60 minutes. Remove from heat and let the rice stand, covered, for 10 minutes to absorb any remaining liquid. Transfer the rice to a large salad bowl.

2. In a small bowl, whisk together the olive oil, vinegar, salt, and pepper, then pour over the warm rice grains and mix well.

3. Mix in the tomatoes, scallions, and corn kernels. Adjust the seasoning. Add the almonds, toss, and serve on lettuce greens.

Soups

Barley Vegetable Soup

This is the kind of earthy soup that sustained our ancestors. And although we are more familiar with barley as an ingredient in mushroom soup, I think you will like it with the lima beans and root vegetables. A grating of good Parmesan cheese on the finished soup would not be amiss.

2 tablespoons extra-virgin olive oil

1 large onion, finely chopped

3 carrots, cut into small dice

3 parsnips, cut into small dice

1 celery rib, cut into small dice

1 leek, white and pale green parts, sliced into thin rounds

6 garlic cloves, finely chopped

2 bay leaves

2 teaspoons fresh thyme leaves, or 1 teaspoon dried thyme

3 quarts water

2 Knorr vegetable bouillon cubes

1 cup pearl barley (see page 162)

1 10-ounce package frozen baby lima beans, thawed

3 tablespoons barley miso

Salt, if needed

Freshly ground black pepper, to taste

$\frac{1}{4}$ cup finely chopped fresh dill

$\frac{1}{4}$ cup finely chopped fresh parsley

1. Heat the oil in a soup pot over medium heat. Add the onion and sauté, stirring frequently, until it begins to turn golden brown, about 10 minutes. Add the carrots, parsnips, celery, leek, garlic, bay leaves, and thyme. Cook, stirring, for 5 minutes longer.

2. Add the water, bouillon cubes, and barley. Bring the soup to a boil, reduce heat to a simmer, and cook at a gentle simmer for 30 minutes. Add the lima beans and

continue cooking for another 15 or 20 minutes, until the barley is tender. Turn off the heat.

3. In a small bowl, add $\frac{1}{2}$ cup soup to the miso. Stir until the mixture is smooth and return to the pot. Taste and add a little salt if necessary. Season with freshly ground black pepper to taste. Remove bay leaves, stir in dill and parsley, and serve.

Soup, as a category, is virtually disappearing from restaurant menus; and I feel that I am being deprived of my birthright, the steaming bowl that comforts and sustains.—Barbara Kafka

White Bean and Roasted Vegetable Soup

You won't go away hungry after eating a bowl of this soup. It is important that the beans are cooked until they are quite soft. Roasting the vegetables, which is an extra step, gives the soup such richness and depth that it is extremely worthwhile.

1 pound dried white cannellini or navy beans

2 tablespoons olive oil

2 large onions, finely chopped

4 garlic cloves, finely chopped

2 bay leaves

8 cups water

$\frac{1}{2}$ small cabbage, coarsely chopped

1 teaspoon fresh thyme leaves, or $\frac{1}{2}$ teaspoon dried thyme

1 small dried hot chili pepper

1 28-ounce can tomatoes, drained and chopped

Olive oil–flavored nonstick cooking spray

3 large carrots, peeled and cut into $\frac{1}{2}$-inch pieces

6 parsnips, peeled and cut into $\frac{1}{2}$-inch pieces

1 medium butternut squash, peeled, seeded, and cut into $1\frac{1}{2}$-inch cubes

1 teaspoon salt, or more to taste

Freshly ground black pepper, to taste

2 tablespoons fresh lemon juice

1 teaspoon brown sugar (optional)

$\frac{1}{2}$ cup finely chopped fresh parsley

1. Pick over the beans to remove any stones or grit. Soak the beans overnight in plenty of water to cover them, or place them in a large pot with 8 cups of water, and bring to a boil. Boil, uncovered, for 2 minutes. Remove from heat, cover, and let stand for 1 to 2 hours. Drain the beans and rinse them.

2. Heat the olive oil in the bottom of a large heavy pot over medium heat and add the onions. Cook, stirring, for 8 to 10 minutes, until the onions begin to color. Add the garlic and bay leaves and cook, stirring, for another minute. Add the water, beans, cabbage, thyme, and chili pepper. Bring to a boil and immediately reduce heat to a very gentle simmer. Partially cover the pot and let simmer while you prepare the remaining vegetables.

3. Preheat oven to 400°F.

4. Spread the carrots, parsnips, and butternut squash in a single layer in a nonstick roasting pan. (Or spray the insides of a regular roasting pan with olive oil–flavored nonstick spray). Spray the vegetables lightly with olive oil–flavored nonstick spray and roast them in the preheated oven for 30 to 40 minutes, until the vegetables begin to caramelize. Turn the vegetables over with a spatula halfway through the roasting time. Remove vegetables from the oven and add them to the cooking beans. Add more water if the soup is very thick. Continue cooking at a gentle simmer for another hour, until the beans are very soft.

5. Season the soup with salt and black pepper to taste. Stir in the lemon juice and taste the soup. It should have a pleasant sweetness from the caramelized vegetables, tempered by the sourness of the lemon juice and some heat from the chili pepper. If you feel it wants more sweetness, add the brown sugar.

6. Remove bay leaves, stir in the parsley, and serve.

She pointed to the flushed and irritable children. See, they were all sick. They were not getting the proper food. "What is the proper food?" Pilon demanded. "Beans," she said. "There you have something you can trust, something that will not go right through you."
—John Steinbeck, *Tortilla Flat*

Very Hearty Corn Chowder

I first ate a corn chowder like this one in Taos, New Mexico, at The Historic Taos Inn. I've since created this recipe, which can be made year-round thanks to good quality frozen corn kernels. It is, indeed, a very hearty chowder and needs only some good bread and perhaps a salad to round out the meal.

1 tablespoon unsalted butter

1 tablespoon extra-virgin olive oil

2 large onions, finely chopped

2 carrots, diced

1 celery rib, diced

1 red bell pepper, ribbed, seeded, and finely chopped

3 jalapeño peppers, ribbed, seeded, and finely chopped

8 garlic cloves, finely minced

$\frac{1}{4}$ cup finely minced fresh parsley

1 tablespoon fresh oregano

2 teaspoons fresh thyme leaves, or 1 teaspoon dried thyme

2 teaspoons paprika

$\frac{1}{4}$ teaspoon cayenne (or to taste)

6 cups vegetable broth or water

3 large potatoes (about $1\frac{1}{2}$ pounds), peeled and diced

2 large yams or sweet potatoes (about 1 pound), peeled and diced

3 corn tortillas, cut into fine julienne

2 cups fresh or frozen corn kernels

1 4-ounce can mild green chilies, drained and finely chopped

1 to 2 cups soy milk or whole milk

1 teaspoon salt, or to taste

Freshly ground black pepper, to taste

GARNISH

2 limes, quartered

$\frac{1}{2}$ cup finely chopped fresh cilantro

1. Heat the butter and olive oil in a soup pot over medium heat. Add the onions and cook, stirring frequently, for 10 minutes, until the onions begin to color. Add the carrots, celery, peppers, garlic, parsley, oregano, thyme, paprika, and cayenne. Cook for another 5 minutes, stirring frequently.

2. Add the broth or water, potatoes, yams, and tortillas. Cook, uncovered, over low heat, at a gentle simmer for about 20 minutes, until the potatoes are just cooked.

3. Add the corn kernels, green chilies, and some soy or regular milk if the soup looks too thick. It should be a consistency you like. Cook 5 minutes longer and remove from heat. Season with salt and freshly ground black pepper to taste.

4. Serve in large soup bowls and pass the limes and cilantro for garnishing.

It was a struggle not to accept second or even third helpings of soup and so risk having no appetite left for the dishes to follow. This is one of the dangers of good soup.—Elizabeth David

Split Pea Soup with Carrots, Dill, and Potatoes

6 main-course servings, with possible leftovers

Everybody loves pea soup, but wait until you try this version. The chipotle peppers add spice and a mysterious smokiness. The chunks of carrots and potatoes add needed color and texture. And the dill brings the flavors together into a harmonious whole.

2 cups yellow or green split peas

$3\frac{1}{2}$ quarts water

1 large onion, finely chopped

4 carrots, diced

2 celery ribs, diced

1 or 2 chiles chipotles in adobo sauce (optional)

$\frac{1}{4}$ cup finely chopped fresh parsley

$\frac{1}{4}$ cup finely chopped fresh dill

1 tablespoon fresh thyme leaves, or 1 teaspoon dried thyme

1 bay leaf

3 medium potatoes, peeled, cubed, and held in cold water to cover until needed

2 teaspoons salt, or to taste

Freshly ground black pepper, to taste

1. Pick over the peas to remove any stones or debris. Rinse them under cold running water and place in a large soup pot together with the cold water. Bring to a boil and skim off any foam that rises to the surface. Reduce heat to low and add the onion, carrots, celery, the chipotle pepper, half the parsley, half the dill, thyme, and bay leaf. Cook the soup at a gentle simmer for $1\frac{1}{2}$ hours.

2. Stir the soup, add the potatoes, and some additional water if it is getting too thick. Season with salt and pepper, and continue cooking for another hour, until the potatoes are cooked through and the peas are soft. Taste and adjust the seasoning. Garnish with remaining parsley and dill, and serve.

There is nothing like a bowl of hot soup, its wisp of aromatic steam teasing the nostrils into quivering anticipation.—Louis P. de Gouy

Ribollita (Tuscan Bread Soup)

This classic Italian bread soup is a nutritional powerhouse, a vegetarian's dream come true, and my favorite meal in a bowl on a wintry night.
It might seem, at first glance, like an elaborate production. But it's really a very easy and flexible recipe. You can leave out some of the greens or substitute others and, conveniently, this soup tastes best if made a day or two before serving.

1 cup dried cannellini beans, picked over and washed, soaked in water
  overnight
1 bay leaf
1 dried red chili pepper (optional)
1 teaspoon salt, or to taste
1 tablespoon olive oil
2 medium onions, chopped
2 celery ribs, diced
3 medium carrots, peeled and diced
6 large garlic cloves, finely chopped or pushed through a garlic press
1 28-ounce can whole tomatoes, drained and coarsely chopped
4 medium potatoes, peeled and diced
3 small zucchini, diced (optional)
1 bunch Swiss chard, stalks removed, leaves thoroughly washed, drained, and
  chopped
1 bunch kale, stalks removed, leaves thoroughly washed, drained, and chopped
$\frac{1}{2}$ small cabbage, finely chopped
$\frac{1}{2}$ pound green beans, trimmed and cut into 1-inch pieces (optional)
$\frac{1}{2}$ cup finely chopped parsley
1 tablespoon fresh thyme leaves, or 1 teaspoon dried thyme
2 or 3 additional garlic cloves, pushed through a garlic press
Salt and freshly ground black pepper, to taste
Red pepper flakes, to taste
1 loaf crusty country-style bread, cut into 12 slices

Additional garlic clove, cut in half
Additional parsley for garnish

1. Drain the beans and combine with 1 quart water in a large soup pot. Bring to a boil and boil the beans hard for 1 to 2 minutes. Reduce heat to a low simmer, add the bay leaf and chili pepper, and cook, partially covered, for about 2 hours, until the beans are tender. Add the salt and stir. Remove half the beans with a slotted spoon and purée them along with a little of the cooking liquid in a food processor. Set the purée aside and let the remaining beans cool in the cooking liquid. Remove the bay leaf and chili pepper.

2. Heat the oil in a large soup pot or Dutch oven (6-quart capacity) over low heat. Add the onion, celery, and carrots, and sauté for about 10 minutes, until the onions have wilted. Stir in the garlic and sauté for 2 minutes longer. Add the tomatoes, potatoes, the whole cooked beans and their broth, the zucchini, Swiss chard leaves, kale leaves, cabbage, green beans, parsley, and thyme. Add enough water to cover and bring to a simmer. Cover and simmer gently for 1 hour.

3. Add more water if necessary, 1 cup at a time. Stir in the puréed beans and additional garlic, mix well, and season to taste with salt, freshly ground black pepper, and red pepper flakes. At this point the soup can be cooled and refrigerated until ready to serve. It will keep in the refrigerator for up to 5 days, and improve in flavor along the way. The soup can also be frozen for up to 3 months.

4. To serve, toast the bread and rub each piece with garlic. Place 2 slices in the bottom of a large soup bowl, pour hot soup over the bread, garnish with parsley, and serve.

Tuscans like their soup rich and thick—with or without bread. Bread was the one element always present in the Tuscan kitchen, but fantasy raised a simple peasant soup to the level of culinary art. Bread may have filled the stomach, but Tuscan imagination provided the good taste. . . . Today when you eat a bread soup in Tuscany you know that you are eating an original peasant dish.—Pino Luongo

Kale and Potato Soup

4 to 6 servings

This soup is a vegetarian version of the Portuguese classic called caldo verde. *It is so tasty and satisfying that no one will miss the sausage. Serve this with a good country bread, a little bit of cheese, and a salad.*

1 bunch kale (about 1 pound)
2 tablespoons extra-virgin olive oil
1 large onion, coarsely chopped
12 garlic cloves, peeled and thinly sliced
$\frac{1}{2}$ teaspoon crushed hot red pepper flakes, or more to taste
1 bay leaf
1 teaspoon salt
6 medium Yukon Gold or red potatoes ($1\frac{1}{2}$ pounds), peeled and chopped into
    small cubes
8 cups water
Freshly ground black pepper, to taste

1. Cut the kale leaves off their stems. Discard the stems and wash and dry the leaves. Chop the leaves into small pieces and set aside.

2. Heat the oil in the bottom of a soup pot over medium heat. Add the onion, garlic, red pepper flakes, and bay leaf. Cook, stirring frequently, for about 10 minutes, until the onion just starts to take on some color.

3. Add the salt, kale, potatoes, and water. Bring to a boil, reduce heat to a gentle simmer, and cook, covered, for about 30 minutes, until the potatoes are soft.

4. At this point you'll have to decide on the texture you want. You can leave it as is for a rustic chunky texture (this is my favorite), mash it a few times with a potato masher, or purée it in a food mill or blender.

5. Taste for seasoning, add black pepper to taste, and serve.

What I say is that, if a fellow really likes potatoes, he must be a pretty decent sort of fellow.—A. A. Milne

32   The One-Dish Vegetarian

Okra-Corn Gumbo

This most untraditional gumbo is loosely based on the recipe for okra soup in Marion Morash's indispensable (at least in my kitchen) book, The Victory Garden Cookbook. *It is a hearty, stewlike soup that needs only a loaf of good bread to make a complete meal.*

3 tablespoons unsalted butter or vegetable oil

1 large onion, finely chopped

1 green bell pepper, cored, seeded, and chopped

3 jalapeño peppers, cored, seeded, and finely chopped

1 celery rib, finely chopped

8 garlic cloves, finely chopped

2 chiles chipotles in adobo sauce, chopped (optional)

2 teaspoons fresh thyme leaves, or 1 teaspoon dried thyme

1 teaspoon paprika

$\frac{1}{4}$ teaspoon cayenne

1 bay leaf

2 cups thinly sliced okra, or 1 10-ounce package frozen sliced okra

1 28-ounce can tomatoes, chopped and with their juices

1 tablespoon Worcestershire sauce

8 cups hot vegetable broth or water

$\frac{3}{4}$ cup long-grain rice

2 cups fresh or frozen corn kernels

Freshly ground black pepper, to taste

1 teaspoon Tabasco or other hot sauce, or to taste

1 teaspoon salt, or to taste

6 scallions, finely chopped, some green part included

1. In a heavy-bottomed soup pot or Dutch oven, heat the butter or oil over medium heat. Add the onion, peppers, celery, garlic, chiles chipotles, thyme, paprika, cayenne, and bay leaf. Cook, stirring constantly, for 5 to 10 minutes, until the vegetables have wilted.

2. Add the okra and cook, stirring, for about 5 minutes, until some of the stickiness starts to go away. Add the tomatoes and their juices, Worcestershire, and the broth or water. Bring to a boil, add the rice, stir, and reduce heat to a simmer. Cover and simmer for 20 minutes. Add the corn kernels and simmer for another 10 minutes.

3. Season to taste with freshly ground black pepper, Tabasco, and more salt if necessary. Add the scallions and serve while hot.

Variations
- Add any number of other vegetables to the gumbo, such as baby lima beans, smoky grilled eggplant, or coarsely chopped mustard greens or kale.
- Omit the rice from the soup and serve it over a mound of cooked long-grain rice.

The great dish of New Orleans, and which it claims the honor of having invented, is the Gumbo. There is no dish which at the same time so tickles the palate, satisfies the appetite, furnishes the body with nutriment sufficient to carry on the physical requirements, and costs so little, as a Creole gumbo. It is dinner in itself, being soup, pièce de résistance and vegetable in one. Healthy, not heating to the stomach, and easy of digestion, it should grace every table.—William Coleman

Another view of okra . . .
Lady's fingers, the five-sided pods of Hibiscus esculentes, are the most elegant of vegetables—as their name suggests. They could be classed with Chinese artichokes for beauty of form.—Jane Grigson's Vegetable Book

Summer Corn Soup

4 main-course servings

This soup captures the fresh, sweet corn flavors of late summer or early fall. It is a soup to prepare when you return from the farmstand, and it makes a very pleasant lunch or light supper, supported by some bread and perhaps a plate of sliced tomatoes.

2 tablespoons unsalted butter

1 large onion, finely chopped

1 sweet red pepper, seeded and diced

3 very small zucchini, quartered lengthwise and diced

1 teaspoon ground toasted cumin (see page 172)

$\frac{1}{4}$ teaspoon cayenne

1 pound boiling potatoes, peeled and diced

2 cups light vegetable stock or water (see page 156)

2 cups reduced fat soy milk or low-fat milk

2 cups fresh corn kernels

$\frac{1}{2}$ teaspoon salt, or more to taste

Freshly ground black pepper, to taste

2 tablespoons finely chopped fresh parsley

2 tablespoons chopped cilantro

1. Heat the butter over low heat in a heavy saucepan. Add the onion, sweet pepper, and zucchini, and cook slowly for about 10 minutes, until the vegetables are tender. Stir in the cumin and cayenne.

2. Add the potatoes, stock, and milk to the saucepan. Bring to a simmer and cook, covered, until potatoes are very tender, about 20 minutes.

3. Stir in the corn, bring to a simmer, and cook for 5 minutes. Season to taste with salt and pepper. Stir in the parsley and cilantro, and serve.

People have tried and they have tried, but sex is not better than sweet corn.—Garrison Keillor

Soups 35

Black Bean Soup

There are so many versions of this American classic soup, and if you love black beans, as I do, they are all good. I like to make mine zippy with plenty of garlic and heat from chilies. The chiles chipotles that come canned in an adobo sauce are particularly good here because they add a dimension of smokiness to the soup. A lovely garnish for the soup comes from a tablespoon or two of fresh salsa. A recipe for the salsa follows the soup recipe. You can, of course, substitute a good quality, prepared salsa.

2 tablespoons extra-virgin olive oil

1 large onion, coarsely chopped

2 celery ribs, finely chopped

2 carrots, finely chopped

6 to 8 cloves garlic, finely chopped

1 or 2 chiles chipotles in adobo sauce, coarsely chopped, or $\frac{1}{2}$ teaspoon hot red pepper flakes

2 bay leaves

1 teaspoon dried oregano

1 teaspoon whole cumin

10 cups water

2 cups black beans, soaked for 4 to 8 hours in plenty of cold water (see page 168)

1 or 2 large vegetarian bouillon cubes

Salt, to taste

Freshly ground black pepper, to taste

Hickory smoke flavoring (optional)

$\frac{1}{2}$ cup fresh cilantro leaves

2 limes or lemons, quartered

1. Heat the olive oil in a large soup pot over medium heat. Add the onion and cook, stirring, for 2 minutes, until it wilts. Add the celery, carrots, and garlic, and cook, stirring, for 2 minutes. Add the chiles chipotles or red pepper flakes, bay leaves, oregano, cumin, and water.

2. Drain the beans, rinse them under cold water, and add them to the soup. Bring the soup to a boil and boil on high heat for 1 minute. Reduce heat to low and simmer, uncovered, for $2\frac{1}{2}$ to 3 hours, until the beans are soft and partially disintegrated.

3. Add the bouillon cubes, salt, and freshly ground black pepper to taste. Add a drop or two of hickory smoke flavoring. Simmer for 30 minutes to blend seasonings. Remove the bay leaves. Use a hand blender to purée the soup to the consistency you like. Or transfer half the soup to a blender, purée it, and return to the soup in the pot.

4. Serve in deep bowls, garnished with cilantro leaves. Pass the lemon or lime wedges separately. Pass a bowl of salsa at the table.

Salsa

about 2 cups

1 small onion, finely chopped
4 ripe tomatoes, coarsely chopped
1 or 2 fresh jalapeño peppers, cored, seeded, and finely chopped
Salt, to taste
$\frac{1}{4}$ cup finely chopped fresh cilantro leaves
2 tablespoons freshly squeezed lime juice

Combine all the ingredients in a small bowl and stir well, to blend.

When you have four hundred pounds of beans in the house, you need have no fear of starvation. Other things, delicacies such as sugar, tomatoes, peppers, coffee, fish, or meat may come sometimes miraculously, through the intercession of the Virgin, sometimes through industry or cleverness; but your beans are there, and you are safe.—John Steinbeck, *Tortilla Flat*

Many Mushroom Soup
with Barley

In my experience, barley is the most sustaining of all grains. When you've eaten barley, your body relaxes, knowing it won't have to think about food again for quite a long time. The combination of mushrooms with barley in a soup is a classic one, and for good reason. The mushrooms provide a deep, meaty richness of taste to the strong body of the barley. This is a most delicious soup, and I like to splurge a little by buying the greatest variety of mushrooms I can find. If you make the soup the day before serving it, you may have to add more liquid to the soup because the barley goes on expanding as it stands.

$\frac{1}{2}$ cup ($\frac{1}{2}$ ounce) dried mushrooms

2 pounds fresh mushrooms, all one kind or a mixture of chanterelle, morel, shiitake, or porcini

2 tablespoons butter or canola oil

1 large onion, finely chopped

4 garlic cloves, finely minced

$2\frac{1}{2}$ quarts vegetable broth or water

1 cup pearl barley (see page 162)

2 celery ribs, cut into $\frac{1}{2}$-inch-thick slices

2 carrots, cut into $\frac{1}{2}$-inch-thick slices

2 parsnips, cut into $\frac{1}{2}$-inch-thick slices

2 bay leaves

$\frac{1}{2}$ teaspoon dried thyme

Salt, to taste

Freshly ground black pepper, to taste

$\frac{1}{2}$ cup chopped fresh dill

1. Soak the dried mushrooms in 1 cup hot water for 15 minutes. Drain the mushrooms, reserving the soaking liquid, and chop them into fine dice. Strain the re-

served liquid through a paper coffee filter or cheesecloth and add to the vegetable broth or water.

2. Trim away any tough mushroom stems and clean the mushrooms with moist paper towels. Slice or chop the mushrooms and set aside.

3. In a large soup pot, heat the butter or oil over medium heat. Add the onion and garlic, and sauté for 2 minutes, stirring frequently, until onion is limp. Add all the mushrooms and sauté until they turn soft and start to release their moisture, about 5 minutes.

4. Stir in the vegetable broth or water and add the barley, celery, carrots, parsnips, bay leaves, thyme, salt, and freshly ground black pepper. Bring the soup to a boil, reduce heat to a simmer, and cook over low heat, partially covered, for 1 hour, until the barley is quite tender. Taste the soup and adjust the seasoning. Remove bay leaves and stir in the fresh dill.

> Do you have a kinder, more adaptable friend in the food world than soup? Who soothes you when you are ill? Who refuses to leave you when you are impoverished and stretches its resources to give you a hearty sustenance and cheer? Who warms you in the winter and cools you in the summer? Yet who also is capable of doing honor to your richest table and impressing your most demanding guests? . . . Soup does its loyal best, no matter what undignified conditions are imposed upon it. You don't catch steak hanging around when you're poor and sick, do you?—Judith Martin (Miss Manners)

Russian Cabbage Borscht with Beets

Although my mother's borscht was always made with beef stock and had lots of meaty chunks among the vegetables, I like the vegetarian version even better. The flavors of the vegetables ring clear and true and are nicely accented by the sweet and sour tastes.

2 teaspoons butter or canola oil

1 large onion, finely chopped

2 medium leeks, white and pale green parts, thoroughly washed and thinly sliced

1 teaspoon sweet paprika

$2\frac{1}{2}$ quarts water

1 small cabbage (1 to $1\frac{1}{2}$ pounds), cored and finely shredded

1 pound beets (about 5), trimmed, scrubbed, and cut into $\frac{1}{2}$-inch chunks

3 boiling potatoes, peeled and cut into 1-inch chunks

1 tart apple, peeled, cored, and seeded and cut into $\frac{1}{4}$-inch dice

1 large carrot, peeled and finely chopped

1 celery rib, cut into $\frac{1}{4}$-inch dice

6 garlic cloves, finely chopped

$\frac{1}{4}$ cup tomato paste

$\frac{1}{4}$ cup light brown sugar

2 bay leaves

1 tablespoon caraway seeds

Salt, to taste

Freshly ground black pepper, to taste

1 or 2 tablespoons fresh lemon juice

$\frac{1}{3}$ cup chopped fresh parsley, for garnish

$\frac{1}{3}$ cup chopped fresh dill, for garnish

Optional: sour cream or yogurt to pass at the table

1. Heat the butter or oil in a large soup pot over medium heat. Add the onion and leeks, and sauté for 2 minutes. Add the paprika and sauté for 1 minute.

2. Add the water, the cabbage, beets, potatoes, apple, carrot, celery, garlic, tomato paste, sugar, bay leaves, caraway seeds, salt, and pepper. Bring the soup to a boil, reduce heat to a simmer, and cook over low heat for 2 hours. Remove from heat and add 1 tablespoon lemon juice.

3. Taste the soup and adjust the seasonings, adding more salt, sugar, lemon juice to balance the sweet, salty, sour flavors. Stir in the parsley and dill and serve. (This soup tastes even better if refrigerated overnight, reheated, and served.)

> . . . But even better is a borscht, prepared with sugar beets, Ukrainian style, you know the way, my friend. . . . It should be served with sour cream, of course, and a sprinkling of fresh parsley and dill.
> —Anton Chekhov, "The Siren"

Lentil Soup with Spicy Greens

In the winter, I make lentil soup at least once a week and have it around for several days. I serve it for dinner with hearty bread and a salad or some fruit. A sturdy red wine is a great accompaniment. If there is any leftover, I have it for lunch, or as a great pick-me-up after a long walk in the cold.

3 tablespoons extra-virgin olive oil

2 large onions, finely chopped

6 garlic cloves, finely chopped

1 teaspoon ground cumin (see page 172)

1 teaspoon ground turmeric

2 quarts water

2 cups French green lentils (*lentilles du Puy*), picked over and rinsed

2 large carrots, peeled and finely chopped

2 celery ribs, finely chopped

2 bay leaves

$\frac{1}{2}$ teaspoon thyme

1 teaspoon salt, or more to taste

1 tablespoon brown mustard seeds

$\frac{1}{2}$ teaspoon hot red pepper flakes

1 pound mustard greens, Swiss chard, or kale, tough stalks removed, washed, and coarsely chopped

Freshly ground black pepper, to taste

1 to 2 tablespoons fresh lemon juice

1. Heat 2 tablespoons olive oil in a large soup pot over medium heat. Add the onions and sauté, stirring frequently, for about 10 minutes, until the onion turns golden brown. Add the garlic, cumin, and turmeric, and cook, stirring, for another 2 minutes.

2. Add the water, lentils, carrots, celery, bay leaves, thyme, and salt. Bring the soup to a boil, lower the heat to a simmer, and cook over low heat for 30 minutes, stirring occasionally.

3. In a large skillet or sauté pan, heat the remaining tablespoon of olive oil over medium heat. Add the mustard seeds and cook, stirring, until the seeds begin to pop. Add the red pepper flakes and all the greens and cook, stirring, for about 5 minutes, until the greens begin to wilt.

4. Stir the greens into the soup and simmer over low heat for 15 to 20 minutes, until the greens are tender.

5. Taste and adjust the seasonings to your liking, adding additional salt, freshly ground black pepper, and a tablespoon or 2 of lemon juice.

God, how my mouth waters when I think of lentil soup.—Richard Gehman, *The Haphazard Gourmet*

Vegetarian Hot and Sour Soup

4 to 5 servings

I learned to make this great soup from two sources, Ken Hom's Asian Vegetarian Feast *and Madhur Jaffrey's* World of the East Vegetarian Cooking. *I have often served it to guests without mentioning that it is a vegetarian version of this classic Chinese soup, and no one has ever even noticed that the pork is missing.*

$\frac{1}{2}$ ounce tree ear fungus (also called black fungus or cloud ears)

6 Chinese dried black mushrooms

$\frac{1}{3}$ cup dried day lily buds

2 ounces bean thread (transparent) noodles

4 cups vegetable stock (see page 156)

1 tablespoon finely chopped fresh ginger

1 garlic clove, pushed through a garlic press

$\frac{1}{2}$ cup bamboo shoots, cut into thin strips

4 ounces firm tofu, cut into thin strips

$\frac{1}{2}$ teaspoon salt

2 tablespoons red wine vinegar

1 tablespoon soy sauce

$\frac{1}{2}$ teaspoon freshly ground white pepper

1 tablespoon cornstarch

2 teaspoons dark roasted sesame oil

1 egg, lightly beaten

2 scallions, trimmed and thinly sliced

1. Soak the tree ears, mushrooms, and day lily buds in $1\frac{1}{2}$ cups of warm water each, for 30 minutes. Soak the bean thread noodles in a large bowl of warm water for 15 minutes.

2. Place the vegetable stock together with the ginger and garlic in a soup pot over medium-low heat and bring to a simmer.

3. When the noodles are soft, drain them and cut them into 3-inch lengths. This is easily done with a pair of scissors. Add them to the simmering broth. Drain the day lily buds, cut away the hard ends, and add them to the broth. Drain the mushrooms, remove and discard the stems, cut the caps into $\frac{1}{4}$-inch-wide strips, and add them to the broth. Drain the tree ear fungus and rinse under cold running water. If there are any hard bumps, cut them away and discard them. Add them to the broth. Keep the broth at a low simmer.

4. Add the bamboo shoots, tofu, and salt to the soup. Simmer for 5 minutes. Add the vinegar, soy sauce, and white pepper.

5. In a small bowl, mix the cornstarch together with 1 tablespoon cold water, then stir in 1 teaspoon of sesame oil. Stir this mixture into the simmering soup. Simmer, stirring from time to time, 3 to 5 minutes, until the soup thickens slightly.

6. In a small bowl, combine the egg with 1 teaspoon sesame oil, mix with a fork, and pour this into the simmering soup. Use chopsticks, or the straight end of a wooden spoon, to swirl the egg into the soup. Turn off the heat, garnish with scallions, and serve while soup is hot.

Note

Tree ear fungus, Chinese dried black mushrooms, and day lily buds can all be found in Asian markets or by mail order. See mail-order sources, page 173.

Pasta

Farfalle with Many Mushrooms

4 to 5 servings

I like to use a variety of fresh mushrooms in this sauce and I make up the combination as I shop at the market. The very flavorful shiitake mushrooms are always included, and then I buy what other types I can find. Occasionally, chanterelles or morels find their way into the mix, but usually the combination is made up of shiitakes, cremini, oyster, portobello, and cultivated white mushrooms. Feel free to experiment with what is available to you. Farfalle are lovely bow-tie–shaped pasta, but you can substitute shells, tubes, wagon wheels, or spirals.

2 tablespoons extra-virgin olive oil

1 tablespoon unsalted butter

2 pounds mixed mushrooms, wiped clean, stems removed, and sliced

1 teaspoon salt

Freshly ground black pepper

6 large garlic cloves, finely minced

$\frac{1}{4}$ to $\frac{1}{2}$ teaspoon red pepper flakes (optional, but very good)

1 large handful of Italian parsley, finely chopped

$\frac{1}{2}$ cup dry white or red wine

2 tablespoons salt

1 pound farfalle

1 to 2 tablespoons unsalted butter (optional)

Freshly grated Parmesan cheese

1. Place a large pot of water (6 quarts) on high heat to boil for the pasta.

2. While the water is heating, heat the oil and butter in a large sauté pan or skillet. Add the mushrooms and sauté over high heat for about 5 minutes, until the mushrooms start to turn brown around the edges. Toss them occasionally with a metal spatula.

3. Season the mushrooms with salt and pepper, lower the heat to medium, and add the garlic, red pepper flakes, parsley, and wine. Stir well and cook for 5 minutes

longer. Taste for seasoning, adding more salt and pepper if necessary. Turn off the heat but leave the pan on the burner.

4. When the pasta water comes to a boil, add 2 tablespoons salt and the farfalle, or other pasta. Cook for 8 to 10 minutes, tasting for doneness at 7 or 8 minutes, until the pasta is al dente. Scoop out the pasta and place directly into the mushroom sauce. Let some of the cooking water transfer along with the pasta.

5. Turn heat to high under the sauté pan or skillet and toss pasta with the sauce. At this point you can add a tablespoon or two of butter to the sauce if you wish. Serve in pasta bowls, accompanied by freshly grated Parmesan cheese.

So in that part of France and I'm sure in many others as well, and in Poland, Italy, Czechoslovakia and so on, there exists a large invisible community of mushroom-hunters. The concentration of eyes downwards, the careful tread of boots, require peace. Sunday is the occasion. Woods which have been silent most of the week come alive. The crackling of dry twigs announces our presence to all the others whom we cannot see, a more frequent shushing up of dead leaves, then the triumphant shout of our daughter, who has found the first girolles of the day. —Jane Grigson

Wagon Wheels with Zucchini, Beans, and Tomatoes

4 to 5 main-course servings

This is a great pasta meal for midsummer. If you have a garden and a well-stocked pantry, you may not even have to shop.

2 tablespoons olive oil

6 large garlic cloves, finely minced or pushed through a garlic press

1 teaspoon red pepper flakes, or more to taste

6 small zucchini (about 1 pound), cut into 2-inch julienne

$1\frac{1}{2}$ cups vegetable broth

$\frac{1}{2}$ cup finely chopped flat-leafed parsley

Finely chopped zest of 1 lemon

1 12-ounce can cannellini beans, drained and rinsed

1 teaspoon salt

Freshly ground black pepper, to taste

3 tablespoons fresh lemon juice

2 or 3 ripe tomatoes, coarsely chopped

2 tablespoons salt

1 pound wagon wheels

1 cup shredded basil leaves

$\frac{1}{2}$ cup freshly grated Parmesan cheese

1. Place a large pot of water (6 quarts) on high heat to boil for the pasta.

2. In a large sauté pan or skillet, heat the olive oil over medium heat. Add the garlic and red pepper flakes, and sauté for 1 minute. Add the zucchini, tossing with a spatula over high heat for 1 minute. Add the vegetable broth, parsley, and lemon zest. Reduce heat to medium and cook for 5 minutes. Stir in the cannellini beans and cook for another minute. Turn off the heat and season with salt and pepper to taste. Stir in the lemon juice and chopped tomatoes.

3. Salt the boiling water and cook the wagon wheels for 8 to 10 minutes, until they are al dente. Scoop out the pasta and add to sauté pan with vegetables. Let some

of the cooking water transfer along with the pasta. Add the shredded basil and toss well to make sure the wagon wheels are all sauced.

4. Serve in pasta bowls and serve the cheese or bread crumbs.

Ripe vegetables were magic to me. Unharvested, the garden bristled with possibility. I would quicken at the sight of a ripe tomato, sounding its redness from deep amidst the undifferentiated green. To lift a bean plant's hood of heart-shaped leaves and discover a clutch of long slender pods hanging underneath could make me catch my breath. Cradling the globe of a cantaloupe warmed in the sun, or pulling orange spears straight from his sandy soil—these were the keenest of pleasures, and even today in the garden they're accessible to me, dulled only slightly by familiarity.—Michael Pollan

Spaghettini with Tomato-Corn Salsa Cruda

4 or 5 servings

This uncooked sauce can only be made in the height of summer when vine-ripened tomatoes and sweet corn, picked only hours before, are available. White corn, the variety called Silver Queen, for example, is the sweetest and tastiest for this dish. If you cannot get freshly picked corn, simply leave it out and you will be left with the now classic uncooked tomato sauce, which is quite delicious as well. The sauce will have the most flavor if you allow it to stand at room temperature for at least one hour before adding the cooked spaghetti.

3 large garlic cloves, peeled
$1\frac{1}{2}$ teaspoons coarse salt
$\frac{1}{4}$ cup extra-virgin olive oil
4 medium-size very ripe tomatoes
3 ears sweet corn, shucked
Large handful of fresh basil leaves, shredded
Large handful of Italian flat-leaf parsley, finely chopped
Freshly ground black pepper, to taste
2 tablespoons salt
1 pound spaghettini
Freshly grated Parmesan cheese

1. In a mortar, pound the garlic together with the salt to make a paste. If you have no mortar and pestle, push the garlic through a garlic press and use a spoon to mash together with the salt. Transfer to a bowl large enough to hold the cooked spaghettini. Add the olive oil and mix well.

2. Wash the tomatoes and cut them into $\frac{1}{2}$-inch dice. Add tomatoes and their juices to the bowl.

3. Use a small sharp knife to cut away the corn kernels from the cob and add them to the bowl. Add the basil, parsley, and lots of freshly ground black pepper. Mix well, cover with plastic wrap, and let stand at room temperature until pasta is cooked.

You can make this several hours before you cook the pasta, but please, do not refrigerate.

4. Place a large pot of water (6 quarts) on high heat to boil for the pasta. When the water comes to a full boil, add the salt, then add the spaghettini. Cook until al dente, drain, and add the spaghettini to tomato-corn sauce. Toss well to mix and serve in pasta bowls. Serve the cheese separately.

Variations

- Substitute tiny cherry tomatoes. Halve or quarter the tomatoes before adding them to the sauce.
- I like to add a fresh, hot green chili—serrano or jalapeño—finely minced.

From the United States every year a kind friend sent a little packet of sweet-corn seed grown and gathered by his mother. It was a great treat for us. At that time there was no table corn in France. The French grew corn for animals—in the Bugey, for the chickens. When it was known that we were growing it and eating it, they considered us savages. No one was seduced by the young ears we gave them to taste.—Alice B. Toklas

Spaghetti with Caramelized Onions

You come home in the evening, tired unto exhaustion. No one has shopped for dinner. The weather is foul—rain, sleet, snow—there is no question of going out. You pull out the spaghetti pot, fill it with water, put it on the stove. The pantry has some onions, not much else. You slice the onions and sauté them slowly while you chat with your family, read the mail, whatever. An hour later you boil the spaghetti and toss it with the sauce. You've created magic! A delicious dinner out of nothing much.

2 tablespoons olive oil

2 tablespoons butter

3 large onions (about $1\frac{1}{2}$ pounds), sliced very thin

2 teaspoons salt

Freshly ground black pepper, to taste

$\frac{1}{2}$ cup dry white wine

$\frac{1}{2}$ cup finely chopped parsley

2 tablespoons salt

1 pound spaghetti

Freshly grated Parmesan cheese

1. Place a large pot of water (6 quarts) on high heat to boil for the pasta.

2. In a large sauté pan or skillet, heat the olive oil and butter over medium heat. Add the onions, turn the heat to very low, and cook the onions, stirring occasionally for 45 minutes to 1 hour, until the onions have turned golden brown. Be careful not to let the onions burn. They should cook very slowly and evenly, so adjust your heat accordingly.

3. Add salt and plenty of black pepper to the caramelized onions. Because of their sweetness they should be fairly heavily seasoned.

4. Add the wine and raise the heat to high; simmer until most of the wine has evaporated. Add the parsley, stir, and turn off the heat.

5. Add salt to boiling pasta water then add the spaghetti. Cook the spaghetti until it is al dente. Drain the spaghetti and add to the sauté pan with the caramelized onions. Turn on the heat under the pan and toss the spaghetti with the sauce.

6. Serve at once in pasta bowls and serve the cheese separately.

Variations

- Add $\frac{1}{2}$ cup heavy cream after you have added and simmered the wine. Simmer for a few minutes until the sauce has thickened.
- Stir in $\frac{1}{2}$ cup chopped toasted walnuts or toasted pine nuts just before serving.

An onion can make people cry, but there's no vegetable that can make people laugh.—Anonymous

Spaghetti with Roasted Fennel and Tomatoes

4 to 5 servings

This delicious sauce is easy to make and a nice change of pace from ordinary tomato sauce. Fennel helps to soothe any indigestion due to fatigue and stress. At the same time, it perks up the appetite to help you enjoy your meal. Try it for a Friday night dinner to take away the worries of the week.

2 fennel bulbs (about $1\frac{1}{2}$ pounds)

1 large onion, cut in half lengthwise and thinly sliced

12 (or more) garlic cloves, peeled

$\frac{1}{2}$ teaspoon fennel seeds, lightly crushed

$\frac{1}{4}$ cup extra-virgin olive oil

1 teaspoon salt

1 28-ounce can Italian whole tomatoes, drained

Freshly ground black pepper

2 tablespoons salt

1 pound spaghetti

1. Preheat the oven to 375°F.

2. Remove a handful of feathery fronds from the fennel bulbs, chop them into 1-inch-long pieces, and reserve. Cut away the stalks and remove some of the coarse outer layers. Cut the bulbs in half vertically, cut out the cores, and cut them crosswise into $\frac{1}{8}$-inch-thick slices.

3. Place the sliced fennel, onion, garlic cloves, and fennel seeds in a nonreactive roasting pan. Drizzle with olive oil and sprinkle with 1 teaspoon salt. Place in the preheated oven and roast for 20 minutes, until the fennel is almost tender. Stir the vegetables once or twice while they are roasting.

4. Cut each tomato in half lengthwise and add them to the fennel in the roasting pan. Stir and spread out in one layer. Season with lots of freshly ground black pepper. Continue baking for 30 minutes.

5. Bring 6 quarts of water to a boil, add the 2 tablespoons salt and the spaghetti, and cook until al dente. Drain and add the spaghetti to the vegetables in the roasting pan and mix well. Sprinkle with reserved fennel fronds and serve in pasta bowls.

It was in the hollow pith of the giant fennel, *Ferrula communis*, that Prometheus concealed a lump of live charcoal broken from the torch he lit at the fiery chariot of the sun, defying Zeus, and brought fire to mankind.—Patience Gray, *Honey from a Weed*

Penne with Broccoli, Red Pepper, and Garlic

This recipe is one of my all-time favorites. I prepare it at least once a week all winter long. The ingredients are easily available at a time of year when good fresh produce is hard to come by. And, in minutes, you can prepare a meal that is not only delicious but provides a gold mine of vitamins and minerals. In my book, this is the best kind of health insurance.

$\frac{1}{4}$ cup extra-virgin olive oil

6 to 8 garlic cloves, finely minced

$\frac{1}{2}$ teaspoon hot red pepper flakes, or more to taste

2 red bell peppers, seeded, cored, and cut into $\frac{1}{2}$-inch dice

1 cup finely chopped parsley

1 vegetarian bouillon cube, dissolved in 1 cup hot water

2 tablespoons salt

3 heads broccoli, trimmed, florets cut into bite-size pieces, stalks peeled and cut on the diagonal into bite-size pieces

1 pound penne

Freshly ground black pepper

Freshly grated Parmesan cheese

1. Place a large pot of water (6 quarts) on high heat to boil for the pasta.

2. In a large sauté pan or skillet, heat the olive oil over low heat. Add the garlic, red pepper flakes, and bell peppers, and sauté for 3 minutes, until peppers have become limp. Add the parsley and dissolved bouillon cube, and leave on low heat, stirring occasionally.

3. Add salt to the boiling water and add the broccoli pieces. Boil for 3 minutes, then fish out the broccoli with a slotted spoon or small sieve and add to the sauce in the sauté pan.

4. Add the penne to the boiling water and cook until al dente.

5. Stir the broccoli pieces into the sauce. Season with freshly ground black pepper and turn off the heat. Drain the penne and add to the sauce. Toss well to mix and serve in pasta bowls. Serve the cheese separately.

If fresh broccoli is not cooked properly, then it becomes a big ugly thing, and I don't think that any little kiddie or any big President would like it.—Julia Child

Spaghetti with Tomato and Arugula Sauce

Here is a truly one-dish meal in which you eat your salad mixed right into the spaghetti sauce. Actually, the arugula is lightly steamed by heat from the hot spaghetti and adds a delicious sharp flavor to the tomato sauce. You can leave out the pine nuts if you don't have them, but they do add a nice texture and resiny flavor to the dish.

$\frac{1}{4}$ cup extra-virgin olive oil

6 to 8 garlic cloves, finely minced

$\frac{1}{2}$ teaspoon hot red pepper flakes, or more to taste

1 28-ounce can whole tomatoes, drained and coarsely chopped

1 teaspoon salt

$\frac{1}{2}$ teaspoon sugar

Freshly ground black pepper

Large handful of fresh basil leaves, shredded

1 sprig fresh oregano

2 tablespoons salt

1 pound spaghetti

2 bunches fresh arugula

$\frac{1}{2}$ cup lightly toasted pine nuts

Freshly grated Parmesan cheese

1. In a large sauté pan or skillet, heat the olive oil over low heat. Add the garlic and red pepper flakes, and sauté for 1 minute. Add the tomatoes, salt, sugar, freshly ground black pepper to taste, basil leaves, and oregano. Cook over medium heat for 10 to 15 minutes, until the sauce becomes thick and flavorful. Taste for seasoning and add more salt and pepper, if necessary.

2. Place a large pot of water (6 quarts) on high heat to boil for the pasta.

3. When the water comes to a boil, add the salt and spaghetti, and cook until the spaghetti is al dente.

4. While the spaghetti is cooking, trim away the thick stems of the arugula, wash and dry the leaves, and place them in a serving bowl with a little drizzle of olive oil. Drain the spaghetti, add to the bowl, and toss with the arugula. Add the tomato sauce and pine nuts and toss again. Serve in pasta bowls and serve the cheese separately.

There is an inevitable ritual about serving and eating spaghetti . . . eaten as it should be, in varying degrees of longness and a fine uniformity of writhing limpness and buttery richness and accompanying noisy sounds. —M.F.K. Fisher

Pasta Shells with Lentils and Spinach

Here's a nice variation on Esau's pottage of lentils. The golden onions add a terrific sweet flavor to the cooked lentils, while the spinach adds a nice texture and color to the dish. While you can use any small pasta shape, the shells are particularly nice because they provide a perfect hiding place for the lentils.

1 cup lentils
1 carrot, finely chopped
2 or 3 celery leaves, finely chopped
$\frac{1}{4}$ cup extra-virgin olive oil
2 large onions, finely chopped
$\frac{1}{2}$ teaspoon dried thyme
1 10-ounce package frozen chopped spinach, thawed
1 teaspoon salt, or more to taste
Freshly ground black pepper
2 tablespoons salt
1 pound small pasta shells
$\frac{1}{2}$ cup finely minced fresh parsley
Freshly grated Parmesan cheese

1. In a medium-size saucepan, cook the lentils in 1 quart water together with the carrot and celery leaves. Cook for 15 to 20 minutes, until the lentils are almost tender. Drain the lentils but reserve the cooking water.

2. While the lentils are cooking, heat the olive oil in a large sauté pan or skillet. Add the onions and thyme, and cook, stirring occasionally, over medium heat for 10 to 12 minutes, until the onions are golden brown.

3. Add the lentils to the onions along with 1 cup of the reserved lentil broth. Squeeze excess moisture from the spinach and add to the lentils and onions. Season with 1 teaspoon salt and pepper to taste. Simmer over low heat while the pasta cooks.

4. Bring a large pot of water (6 quarts) to a boil. Add the 2 tablespoons salt and pasta shells. Cook until the shells are al dente. Drain the pasta shells and add them to the lentil sauce. Toss well. Add some more of the reserved lentil cooking liquid if the sauce seems too dry. Add parsley, mix well, and serve in pasta bowls.

5. Serve the cheese separately.

Fusilli with Broccoli and Peanut Sauce

4 to 5 servings

Here's a delicious reminder that not all pasta dishes are Italian. This is a hybrid recipe borrowing ingredients and techniques from Italy (pasta and broccoli), China (soy sauce), and North America (peanuts). If you know anyone who still claims to dislike broccoli, this dish will surely change their mind.

$\frac{3}{4}$ cup smooth peanut butter

$\frac{1}{2}$ cup hot water

2 tablespoons soy sauce

2 teaspoons Worcestershire sauce

2 garlic cloves, pushed through a garlic press

$1\frac{1}{2}$ teaspoons sugar

$\frac{1}{2}$ teaspoon cayenne, or more to taste

2 tablespoons salt

1 pound fusilli

1 large bunch broccoli ($\frac{3}{4}$ to 1 pound), trimmed, florets cut into bite-size pieces, stalks peeled and cut on a diagonal into bite-size pieces

$\frac{1}{2}$ cup finely chopped dry roasted peanuts

1. Place a large pot of water (6 quarts) on high heat to boil for the pasta.F

2. In a bowl large enough to hold the finished pasta, whisk together the peanut butter and hot water until smooth. Whisk in the soy sauce, Worcestershire sauce, garlic, sugar, and cayenne. Taste and adjust the seasonings to balance out the sweet and hot flavors.

3. Salt the boiling water and add the fusilli. Boil for about 7 minutes, until the fusilli is almost al dente. Add the broccoli and boil for 2 to 3 minutes longer.

4. Drain the pasta and vegetables and add them to the bowl with the peanut sauce. Toss well and serve in pasta bowls. Pass the chopped peanuts for garnishing.

Variations

- Substitute any other shape pasta such as wagon wheels, shells, or penne.
- Try adding a tablespoon of fresh lemon juice or red wine vinegar to the peanut sauce.

When you eat broccoli, you're eating flower buds, a fact that always puts me in mind of the lotus-eaters, rather an exotic association for a good, wholesome, plain-and-simple vegetable.—Maggie Waldron

Linguine with Pesto, Green Beans, and Potatoes

The first time I had this dish was in an Italian restaurant in midtown Manhattan. It was a business lunch with a book editor I had never met before. I kept trying to pay attention to our conversation, but I'm afraid that the greater part of my concentration was taken up by the unusual combination of pesto, linguine, potatoes, and green beans. The pasta was absolutely delicious. Nothing much came of that lunch, but I experimented over the next few weeks and came up with this recipe.

$1\frac{1}{2}$ cups fresh basil leaves, rinsed and patted dry

$\frac{1}{2}$ cup freshly grated Parmesan cheese

$\frac{1}{4}$ cup pine nuts, lightly roasted

2 garlic cloves, peeled

1 teaspoon coarse salt

$\frac{1}{4}$ cup extra-virgin olive oil

3 tablespoons unsalted butter

2 tablespoons salt

1 pound potatoes, preferably Yukon Gold, peeled and cut into $\frac{1}{2}$-inch dice

$\frac{3}{4}$ pound green beans, trimmed and cut into 2-inch lengths

1 pound linguine

Freshly ground black pepper

Freshly grated Parmesan cheese

1. Place a large pot of water (6 quarts) on high heat to boil for the pasta.

2. Place the basil, Parmesan cheese, pine nuts, garlic, salt, olive oil, and butter in the bowl of a food processor fitted with a steel blade. Process until the pesto is evenly blended. Remove the pesto to a small bowl and reserve.

3. When the water comes to a boil, add the salt and the potatoes. Cook the potatoes for 5 to 10 minutes, until they are just tender. Remove with a slotted spoon and place in large serving bowl.

4. Add the green beans to the same boiling water and cook for 3 minutes. Remove with a slotted spoon and add to the potatoes in the bowl.

5. Cook the linguine in the same boiling water until it is al dente. Drain the pasta but reserve 1 cup of the cooking liquid. Add the linguine to the potatoes and green beans.

6. Whisk about $\frac{1}{2}$ cup of the reserved cooking liquid into the pesto. Add the pesto to the linguine and toss well to coat the linguine strands and the vegetables with the sauce. Add more liquid if the sauce seems too dry. Season with freshly ground black pepper and serve. Serve the cheese separately.

Variations
- If you prefer, you can prepare the pesto in the more traditional way by pounding the ingredients in a mortar. Pound the basil, pine nuts, garlic, and salt to a paste. Add the grated cheese and grind the mixture until it is evenly blended. Use a wooden spoon to beat in the olive oil and the butter.

Pounding fragrant things—particularly garlic, basil, parsley—is a tremendous antidote to depression. . . . Pounding these things produces an alteration in one's being—from sighing with fatigue to inhaling with pleasure. The cheering effects of herbs and allium cannot be too often reiterated. Virgil's appetite was probably improved equally by pounding garlic as by eating it.—Patience Gray

Linguine with Spring Vegetables

A lovely dish to make when peas and asparagus are fresh in the markets. You can also add any of the following fresh herbs, if you can find them: thyme, tarragon, chervil, or chives.

2 tablespoons olive oil

2 tablespoons unsalted butter

1 large bunch scallions, trimmed, top half of green parts cut away, and thinly sliced

1 tablespoon grated lemon zest

2 tablespoons salt

2 pounds thin asparagus, tough ends removed, cut into 2-inch lengths

1 cup fresh or frozen peas, thawed

$\frac{1}{2}$ cup heavy cream

1 teaspoon salt

Freshly ground black pepper

1 pound linguine

$1\frac{1}{4}$ cups freshly grated Parmesan cheese, plus additional to pass at the table

$\frac{1}{2}$ cup finely chopped parsley

1. Place a large pot of water (6 quarts) on high heat to boil for the pasta.

2. In a large sauté pan or skillet, heat the olive oil and butter over medium heat. Add the scallions, cook over low heat for 1 minute, and turn off the heat. Stir in the lemon zest.

3. When the water comes to the boil, add the 2 tablespoons salt and add the asparagus. Cook for 2 minutes, remove with a slotted spoon, and transfer to the sauté pan with the scallions. Add the peas, heavy cream, salt, and pepper. Simmer over very low heat while you cook the linguine.

4. Add the linguine to the boiling water and cook until al dente. Drain the linguine and add to the sauce. Add $\frac{1}{4}$ cup freshly grated Parmesan cheese and the parsley. Toss well so that all the linguine is coated with the sauce. Serve in pasta bowls and serve the remaining Parmesan cheese.

> The air pulses with the warm smell of lilac, but as we pass each door, the lilac dominance is subdued by heady wafts of asparagus cooking.
> —Jane Grigson

Buckwheat Pasta with Cabbage and Sage

4 to 5 servings

Pizzocheri is a pasta made from buckwheat that is well known in Italy but not so easily available here. If you can find it in an Italian market, by all means use it. If not, substitute buckwheat soba noodles, which are readily available in health-food stores and Asian markets. Both taste great and have a dense, chewy consistency. This is a hearty dish for a cold winter evening.

3 tablespoons unsalted butter

3 tablespoons extra-virgin olive oil

2 large onions, cut lengthwise and thinly sliced

4 garlic cloves, finely minced

1 to $1\frac{1}{2}$ pounds Savoy cabbage, shredded

8 sage leaves, finely minced

1 teaspoon salt

$\frac{1}{4}$ teaspoon cayenne, or more to taste

Freshly ground black pepper

$\frac{1}{2}$ cup white wine

2 tablespoons salt

1 pound buckwheat soba noodles

$\frac{1}{2}$ cup grated Tallegio or Fontina cheese

Freshly grated Parmesan cheese

1. In a large sauté pan or skillet, heat the butter and olive oil over medium heat. Add the onions and garlic, reduce heat to low, and cook, stirring frequently, for 10 to 15 minutes, until onions start turning golden brown. Add the cabbage, sage, 1 teaspoon salt, cayenne, freshly ground black pepper to taste, and white wine. Stir well, cover and cook for 20 minutes, stirring from time to time, until the cabbage is tender.

2. Place a large pot of water (6 quarts) on high heat to boil for the pasta. When the water comes to a boil, add the 2 tablespoons salt and the buckwheat noodles. Cook for 5 to 6 minutes, until noodles are al dente.

3. Drain the noodles and add them to the cabbage. Add the Tallegio or Fontina cheese and mix well. Serve in pasta bowls and serve the Parmesan cheese separately.

Variations

- Substitute $\frac{1}{2}$ pound brussels sprouts for an equal amount of the Savoy cabbage. Cut away the stem and separate the leaves and cook them together with the cabbage.
- Add a handful of chopped toasted walnuts or chestnuts at the very end.

In the night cabbages catch at the moon, the leaves drip silver, the rows of cabbages are series of little silver waterfalls in the moon.
—Carl Sandburg

Soba Noodles with Mushrooms and Peas

4 to 6 servings

I like to make this Asian-inspired pasta dish with soba noodles, which are made of buckwheat flour. These noodles are considered to be very warming, so they are perfect for a winter evening meal. If you don't have soba noodles on hand, feel free to substitute any other kind of noodles, or even linguine.

2 tablespoons canola or peanut oil

$\frac{1}{2}$ teaspoon chili paste with garlic

4 garlic cloves, finely chopped

2 teaspoons freshly grated ginger

8 ounces shiitake mushrooms, stems removed, caps thinly sliced

1 large red bell pepper, cored, seeded, and thinly sliced

1 small head bok choy, cut into $\frac{1}{2}$-inch slices

$\frac{1}{2}$ cup vegetable or mushroom broth or water

8 ounces sugar snap peas, strung and cut in half crosswise

2 tablespoons soy sauce

2 tablespoons seasoned rice vinegar

1 pound soba noodles

1 tablespoon dark roasted sesame oil

$\frac{1}{3}$ cup chopped cashews

1. Place a large pot of water (6 quarts) on high heat to boil for the noodles.

2. In a large sauté pan or skillet, heat the oil over medium heat. Add the chili paste with garlic, the chopped garlic, and ginger. Cook, stirring, for 30 seconds. Add the mushrooms, red bell pepper, and bok choy. Cook, stirring, for about 5 minutes.

3. Add the vegetable broth or water and the sugar snap peas. Simmer on low heat for about 5 minutes, until the peas are tender but retain some bite. Stir in the soy sauce and rice vinegar. Turn off the heat.

4. When the water comes to a boil, add the soba noodles and cook for 8 to 10 minutes, until the noodles are tender. Drain and add the noodles to the vegetables in the sauté pan. Toss and stir until well mixed. Turn heat on high, add the sesame oil, and cook for 1 minute, stirring continuously. Serve in pasta bowls garnished with chopped cashews.

Pasta was born, in the form we recognize—round, flat, spaghetti-like—in Northern China around 100 B.C., when the Chinese began to employ techniques for large-scale flour grinding. A collection of recipes from the sixth century gives instructions for molding two lengths of flat noodles by hand, one "as thin as a scallion leaf."
—Bruce Cost's *Asian Ingredients*

Risotto
& Other Rice and
Grain Dishes

Risotto with Tomatoes and Baby Lima Beans

This is a lovely risotto to prepare at the height of summer, when tomatoes are ripe and flavorful and fresh herbs are to be had from the garden or the market. Serve the risotto in large soup bowls and round out the meal with a green salad and a crusty bread.

1 10-ounce package frozen baby lima beans, thawed

7 cups light vegetable broth or water

3 tablespoons extra-virgin olive oil

1 tablespoon unsalted butter

2 large shallots, finely minced

2 garlic cloves, finely minced

2 cups arborio rice

1 cup white wine

4 ripe tomatoes, cored and finely chopped

1 tablespoon fresh thyme leaves or fresh oregano leaves

2 tablespoons finely minced fresh parsley

$\frac{1}{2}$ teaspoon salt (omit if the broth is salty)

Freshly ground black pepper, to taste

$\frac{1}{2}$ cup shredded basil leaves

2 tablespoons unsalted butter (optional)

$\frac{1}{2}$ cup freshly grated Parmesan cheese, plus more to serve at the table

1. In a small pot, or in the microwave, steam the baby lima beans for about 5 minutes, until they are tender. Set aside until needed.

2. In a saucepan, bring the broth or water to a simmer. Keep the liquid at a bare simmer while you proceed with the risotto.

3. In a heavy 4-quart casserole, heat the oil and butter over medium heat. Add the shallots and garlic, and sauté for 2 to 3 minutes, until softened, but not colored. Add the rice and cook, stirring with a wooden spoon, for about 2 minutes, until the rice

is well coated. When the grains become slightly translucent, add the wine, tomatoes, thyme or oregano leaves, parsley, salt, and pepper. Stir until the liquid is completely absorbed.

4. Add 1 cup hot broth or water, stirring frequently, until the liquid is almost absorbed. Continue adding a little over $\frac{1}{2}$ cup of liquid at a time, stirring until each is almost completely absorbed. Adjust the heat so that the risotto is always at a gentle simmer. After 10 minutes, stir in the baby lima beans and continue adding the broth and stirring. After another 6 to 8 minutes of cooking time, the rice should be pleasantly al dente and creamy at the same time.

5. Stir in a final $\frac{1}{4}$ cup of remaining broth or water and turn off the heat. Add shredded basil leaves, butter, and Parmesan and stir to combine with the rice. Serve risotto as soon as possible, and serve additional Parmesan cheese at the table.

Have you eaten rice today?—Typical greeting in China

Risotto with Peas and
Sugar Snap Peas

4 main-course servings

This is a risotto for spring and early summer, when both types of peas are available and at their sweetest. The peas are added at the very end and cooked for only a few minutes, leaving them quite crisp and crunchy. A lovely contrast to the creaminess of the rice.

7 cups vegetable broth or water

3 tablespoons unsalted butter

1 tablespoon olive oil

2 large shallots, finely chopped, or 1 medium onion, finely chopped

2 garlic cloves, finely chopped

2 cups arborio rice

1 cup white wine

2 tablespoons finely minced parsley

1 tablespoon fresh tarragon

$\frac{1}{2}$ teaspoon salt (omit if the broth is salty)

Freshly ground black pepper, to taste

1 cup fresh or frozen peas

2 cups chopped sugar snap peas

$\frac{1}{2}$ cup freshly grated Parmesan cheese

1. In a saucepan, bring the broth or water to a simmer. Keep the liquid at a bare simmer while you proceed with the risotto.

2. In a heavy 4-quart casserole, heat the butter and oil over medium heat. Add the shallots and garlic and sauté for 2 to 3 minutes, until softened but not colored. Add the rice and cook, stirring with a wooden spoon, for about 2 minutes, until the rice is well coated. When the grains become slightly translucent, add the wine, parsley, tarragon, salt, and pepper. Stir until the liquid is completely absorbed.

3. Add 1 cup hot broth or water, stirring frequently, until the liquid is almost absorbed, then continue adding a little over $\frac{1}{2}$ cup of liquid at a time, stirring until each

is almost completely absorbed. Adjust the heat so that the risotto is always at a gentle simmer. After 15 minutes, stir in the regular peas and sugar snap peas and continue adding the broth and stirring for another 3 to 5 minutes, until the rice is pleasantly al dente and creamy at the same time.

4. Stir in a final $\frac{1}{4}$ cup of remaining broth or water and turn off the heat. Add the Parmesan and stir to combine with the rice. Serve risotto as soon as possible, and serve additional Parmesan cheese at the table.

The highly glutinous arborio rice—the quintessential risotto grain—is grown in Italy's Po River Valley, which runs through the Piedmont, Lombardy, Emilia, and Veneto regions. This medium grain rice produces risotto that is creamy on the outside and al dente—firm to the bite—on the inside.—Patricia Wells

Risotto with Butternut Squash and Sage

All the recipes that I have seen for this wonderful risotto call for cooking the butternut squash in a little water or broth, or along with the rice in the risotto. I prefer to roast the squash cubes in the oven before adding them to the risotto. Oven roasting intensifies the sweet flavor of the squash, as it does with all other vegetables.

1 medium butternut squash (about $1\frac{1}{2}$ pounds), peeled, seeded, and cut into $\frac{1}{2}$-inch cubes

1 tablespoon olive oil

18 sage leaves, 12 left whole, 6 leaves finely shredded

$\frac{1}{2}$ teaspoon salt

Freshly ground black pepper, to taste

7 cups vegetable broth or water

3 tablespoons unsalted butter

1 tablespoon extra-virgin olive oil

1 medium onion, finely chopped

2 cups arborio rice

1 cup dry white wine

$\frac{1}{2}$ cup freshly grated Parmesan cheese

1. Preheat the oven to 350°F.

2. Toss the squash pieces together with 1 tablespoon olive oil. Put them in a baking pan with 12 whole sage leaves and season with salt and pepper. Roast for 15 to 20 minutes, turning the pieces occasionally with a spatula, until the squash is tender and starting to brown around the edges. Be careful not to burn the squash. Remove from oven and reserve. Discard any sage leaves that are burnt.

3. In a saucepan, bring the broth or water to a simmer. Keep the liquid at a bare simmer while you proceed with the risotto.

4. In a heavy 4-quart casserole, heat 2 tablespoons of the butter and oil over medium heat. Add the onion and shredded sage leaves and cook, stirring, for 2 minutes, until the onion begins to soften. Add the rice and cook, stirring with a wooden spoon, for about 2 minutes, until the rice is well coated. When the grains become slightly translucent, add the wine and cook, stirring, until all the liquid is absorbed.

5. Add 1 cup hot broth or water, stirring frequently, until the liquid is almost absorbed, then continue adding a little over $\frac{1}{2}$ cup of liquid at a time, stirring until each is almost completely absorbed. Adjust the heat so that the risotto is always at a gentle simmer. After 15 minutes, stir in the roasted squash and continue adding the broth and stirring for another 3 to 5 minutes, until the rice is pleasantly al dente and creamy at the same time.

6. Stir in a final $\frac{1}{4}$ cup of remaining broth or water and turn off the heat. Add shredded basil leaves, 1 tablespoon butter, and Parmesan and stir to combine with the rice. Serve risotto as soon as possible, and serve additional Parmesan cheese at the table.

As for ourselves, risotto fits most easily into the way we eat when it is the meal, not just an accompaniment.—John and Matt Lewis Thorne

Risotto with Zucchini, Corn, and Red Pepper

In this risotto, the vegetables cook together with the rice to make a very flavorful dish. If corn is not in season, by all means substitute a 10-ounce package of frozen corn kernels that have been thawed.

7 cups vegetable broth or water

3 tablespoons extra-virgin olive oil

1 medium onion

2 garlic gloves, finely chopped

1 large red bell pepper, cored, seeded, and cut into small dice

2 small zucchini, stems trimmed and cut into small dice

2 cups corn kernels, cut from 4 ears of corn

2 cups arborio rice

1 cups dry white wine

$\frac{1}{2}$ teaspoon salt (omit if the broth is salty)

Freshly ground black pepper

$\frac{1}{4}$ cup finely chopped fresh parsley

$\frac{1}{4}$ cup finely shredded fresh basil

$\frac{1}{2}$ cup freshly grated fresh Parmesan

1. In a saucepan, bring the broth or water to a simmer. Keep the liquid at a bare simmer while you proceed with the risotto.

2. In a heavy 4-quart casserole, heat the oil over medium heat. Add the onion, garlic, red pepper, zucchini, and corn kernels and cook, stirring, for 2 to 3 minutes, until the onion begins to soften. Add the rice and cook, stirring with a wooden spoon, for about 2 minutes, until the rice is well coated. When the grains become slightly translucent, add the wine and cook, stirring, until the liquid is completely absorbed.

3. Add 1 cup hot broth or water, stirring frequently, until the liquid is almost absorbed, then continue adding a little over $\frac{1}{2}$ cup of liquid at a time, stirring until each is almost completely absorbed. Adjust the heat so that the risotto is always at a gentle

simmer. After about 18 minutes, the rice should be pleasantly al dente and creamy at the same time.

4. Stir in a final $\frac{1}{4}$ cup of remaining broth or water and turn off the heat. Add parsley, shredded basil leaves, and Parmesan and stir to combine with the rice. Serve risotto as soon as possible, and serve additional Parmesan cheese at the table.

> No artist can work simply for results; he must also like the work of getting them. Not that there isn't a lot of drudgery in any art—and more in cooking than in most—but that if a man has never been pleasantly surprised at the way the custard sets, or flour thickens, there is not much hope of making a cook of him.—Robert Farrar Capon

Risotto with Tomato Sauce

It was a happy day when I discovered that almost any pasta sauce can be incorporated into a risotto with marvelous results. Ever since, when I make a pasta sauce that can keep for a while either in the refrigerator or freezer, I make extra to add to a risotto. The tomato sauce below is a wonderfully fresh tasting sauce that takes only 15 minutes to prepare.

TOMATO SAUCE

2 tablespoons unsalted butter

1 tablespoon extra-virgin olive oil

4 garlic cloves, very thinly sliced

$\frac{1}{2}$ teaspoon hot red pepper flakes

1 28-ounce can whole tomatoes, drained and coarsely chopped

2 tablespoons finely chopped fresh parsley

2 tablespoons finely shredded fresh basil

$\frac{1}{2}$ teaspoon salt

$\frac{1}{2}$ teaspoon sugar

RISOTTO

5 to 6 cups vegetable broth or water

4 tablespoons unsalted butter

1 tablespoon extra-virgin olive oil

1 small onion, finely chopped

2 cups arborio rice

$\frac{1}{2}$ cup dry white wine

$\frac{1}{2}$ cup freshly grated Parmesan cheese, plus more for the table

1. Prepare the tomato sauce. Heat the butter and olive oil in a large skillet over medium heat. Add the garlic and red pepper flakes and cook until the garlic just starts to color, about 1 minute. Be careful not to let it burn. Add the tomatoes, parsley, basil, salt, and sugar. Cook over medium heat for 15 minutes, until the sauce has started to thicken. Remove from heat and reserve.

2. In a saucepan, bring the broth or water to a simmer. Keep the liquid at a bare simmer while you proceed with the risotto.

3. In a heavy 4-quart casserole, heat 2 tablespoons of butter and the oil over medium heat. Add the onion and cook, stirring, for 2 minutes, until the onion has softened. Add the rice and cook, stirring with a wooden spoon, for about 2 minutes, until the rice is well coated. When the grains become slightly translucent, add the wine and cook, stirring, until the liquid is completely absorbed.

4. Add 1 cup hot broth or water, stirring frequently, until the liquid is almost absorbed, then continue adding a little over $\frac{1}{2}$ cup of liquid at a time, stirring until each is almost completely absorbed. Adjust the heat so that the risotto is always at a gentle simmer. After about 15 minutes, add the tomato sauce and continue adding the broth and stirring for another 3 to 5 minutes, until the rice is pleasantly al dente and creamy at the same time.

5. Stir in a final $\frac{1}{4}$ cup of remaining broth or water and turn off the heat. Add the remaining 2 tablespoons butter and the Parmesan cheese and stir to combine with the rice. Serve risotto as soon as possible, and serve additional Parmesan cheese at the table.

The customary way to eat risotto is to flatten it on the plate with your fork so that it will cool evenly, and then begin eating it from the outside edge.—Pino Luongo

Green Risotto with Spinach and Watercress

This simple risotto is so good, I could eat it for breakfast, lunch, and dinner, and often do, if I have any leftovers. Do not hesitate to use frozen spinach here, as it works extremely well. Fresh watercress is available year-round in most supermarkets.

1 pound fresh spinach, stems, removed, leaves thoroughly washed

or

1 10-ounce package frozen spinach, thawed

1 bunch watercress, tough stems removed, thoroughly washed and coarsely chopped

$\frac{1}{2}$ teaspoon salt

4 tablespoons unsalted butter

$\frac{1}{4}$ cup heavy cream

7 cups vegetable broth or water

1 medium onion, finely chopped

2 cups arborio rice

1 cup dry white wine

$\frac{1}{2}$ cup freshly grated Parmesan cheese, plus more for the table

1. In a saucepan, combine spinach and watercress with 2 or 3 tablespoons water and salt and cook over high heat for about 5 minutes, until the leaves have wilted. Transfer to the bowl of a food processor, add 1 tablespoon butter and the heavy cream, and process to a purée.

2. In a saucepan, bring the broth or water to a simmer. Keep the liquid at a bare simmer while you proceed with the risotto.

3. In a heavy 4-quart casserole, heat 2 tablespoons of butter over medium heat. Add the onion and cook, stirring, for 2 minutes, until the onion has softened. Add the rice and cook, stirring with a wooden spoon, for about 2 minutes, until the rice is well coated. When the grains become slightly translucent, add the wine and cook, stirring, until the liquid is completely absorbed.

4. Add a scant cup of the hot broth or water, stirring frequently, until the liquid is almost absorbed, then continue adding a little over $\frac{1}{2}$ cup of liquid at a time, stirring until each is almost completely absorbed. Adjust the heat so that the risotto is always at a gentle simmer. After about 15 minutes, add the reserved spinach and watercress and continue adding the broth and stirring for another 3 to 5 minutes, until the rice is pleasantly al dente and creamy at the same time.

4. Add the Parmesan cheese and remaining 1 tablespoon butter and stir to combine with the rice. Serve risotto as soon as possible, and serve additional Parmesan cheese at the table.

Risotto is like a great simmering stew, where a number of elements surrender their individual identity to the greater purpose of a unified flavor. I don't mean that the individual ingredients of a risotto ought to be indistinguishable, but that they are subordinate to the overall effect.—Paul Bertolli

Risotto with Mushrooms and Red Wine

I particularly like to make this risotto in the autumn, when there is a greater variety of fresh mushrooms available. But portobellos, shiitakes, and criminis are around most of the time, which is a blessing, because I like to eat this risotto all year. This is a great dish to serve to people who think that they do not like to eat vegetarian food: No one ever misses the meat when mushrooms abound!

1 ounce dried porcini mushrooms

1 cup very hot water

6 cups vegetable broth or water

4 tablespoons extra-virgin olive oil

6 garlic cloves, finely chopped

$1\frac{1}{2}$ pounds mixed mushrooms (portobello, shiitake, cremini, etc.), cleaned, stems removed, and thinly sliced

1 teaspoon salt

Freshly ground black pepper

$\frac{1}{2}$ cup finely chopped fresh parsley

2 large shallots, finely chopped

2 cups arborio rice

1 cup full-bodied red wine

2 tablespoons butter

$\frac{1}{2}$ cup freshly grated Parmesan cheese, plus more for the table

1. Soak the dried porcini in the hot water for 15 minutes. Drain the porcini, reserving the soaking liquid, and chop them into fine dice. Strain the reserved liquid through a paper coffee filter or cheesecloth and add to the vegetable broth or water for the risotto.

2. Heat 2 tablespoons of olive oil in a large skillet over medium heat. Add the garlic and cook, stirring, for 1 minute. Add all the mushrooms and cook, stirring frequently, for 10 minutes, until the fresh mushrooms are tender. Add the salt, freshly ground black pepper, and parsley. Cook for 2 minutes longer. Remove from heat and set aside.

3. In a saucepan, bring the broth or water to a simmer. Keep the liquid at a bare simmer while you proceed with the risotto.

4. In a heavy 4-quart casserole, heat the remaining 2 tablespoons oil over medium heat. Add the shallots and cook, stirring, for 2 minutes, until the shallots have softened. Add the rice and cook, stirring with a wooden spoon, for about 2 minutes, until the rice is well coated. When the grains become slightly translucent, add the wine and cook, stirring, until the liquid is completely absorbed.

5. Add 1 cup of the hot broth or water, and stir frequently, until the liquid is almost absorbed, then continue adding a little over $\frac{1}{2}$ cup of liquid at a time, stirring until each is almost completely absorbed. Adjust the heat so that the risotto is always at a gentle simmer. After about 15 minutes, add the reserved mushrooms and continue adding the broth and stirring for another 3 to 5 minutes, until the rice is pleasantly al dente and creamy at the same time.

6. Add the butter, Parmesan cheese, salt, and pepper to taste. Stir to combine with the rice. Serve risotto as soon as possible, and serve additional Parmesan cheese at the table.

According to Chinese legend, mushrooms contribute to a long, healthy life. Throughout the Orient, the shiitake is credited with enough curative abilities to make it the ultimate panacea. It's believed to cure everything from cancer to the common cold.—Maggie Waldron

Risotto with Eggplant and Tomatoes

The seductive flavor and texture of eggplant combined with its traditional accompaniments of tomato and mozzarella cheese make for a splendid risotto. I have experimented with replacing some of the fresh mozzarella with smoked mozzarella, with pleasing results.

1 small eggplant (about 1 pound), peeled and cut into 1-inch cubes

4 tablespoons extra-virgin olive oil

4 garlic cloves, finely chopped

$\frac{1}{2}$ teaspoon hot red pepper flakes

2 cups whole canned tomatoes, drained and coarsely chopped

Small handful of basil leaves, finely chopped

Salt, to taste

Freshly ground black pepper, to taste

7 cups vegetable broth

1 small onion, finely chopped

2 cups arborio rice

$\frac{1}{2}$ cup red or white wine

$\frac{3}{4}$ cup diced fresh mozzarella cheese

$\frac{1}{2}$ cup freshly grated Parmesan cheese

1. Preheat the oven to 400°F.

2. Toss the eggplant cubes together with 1 teaspoon olive oil. Spread them out in a single layer on a baking sheet and bake in the oven for about 25 minutes, until they are browned and tender. Remove and reserve.

3. In a sauté pan or skillet, heat $1\frac{1}{2}$ tablespoons of olive oil over medium heat. Add the garlic and red pepper flakes and sauté for 30 seconds. Add the chopped tomatoes and basil. Cook over high heat until the sauce just thickens. Remove from heat, stir in the eggplant, and season to taste with salt and pepper.

4. In a saucepan, bring the vegetable broth to a simmer. Keep the liquid at a bare simmer while you proceed with the risotto.

5. In a heavy 4-quart casserole, heat the remaining olive oil over medium heat. Add the onion and cook, stirring, for 2 minutes, until the onion has softened. Add the rice and cook, stirring with a wooden spoon, for about 2 minutes, until the rice is well coated. When the grains become slightly translucent, add the wine and cook, stirring, until the liquid is completely absorbed.

6. Add 1 cup of hot broth or water, and stir frequently, until the liquid is almost absorbed, then continue adding a little over $\frac{1}{2}$ cup of liquid at a time, stirring until each is almost completely absorbed. Adjust the heat so that the risotto is always at a gentle simmer. After about 18 minutes, add the reserved eggplant and tomato, a final $\frac{3}{4}$ cup of broth, and continue stirring for another 2 to 3 minutes, until the rice is pleasantly al dente and creamy at the same time.

7. Add the mozzarella and Parmesan cheese and stir to combine with the rice. Serve risotto as soon as possible, and serve additional Parmesan cheese at the table.

Eggplant helps lower cholesterol in the nicest possible way: It prevents it from forming if it's a regular part of your diet. Eggplant seems to work by absorbing cholesterol in the intestines so the cholesterol never seems to get into the blood stream where it can clog arteries. Eat eggplant with other fatty foods, and the eggplant will sop up the fats so they can do no harm.—Maggie Waldron, *Cold Spaghetti at Midnight*

Risotto with Cauliflower, Raisins, and Pine Nuts

4 main-course servings

Raisins and pignolis (pine nuts) are often used in dishes from southern Italy, and saffron is the key ingredient of Risotto alla Milanese. The combination of all three ingredients in one risotto makes it something of a mutt, but I can tell you that although it has no proper pedigree, it is very good. The cauliflower goes extremely well with all three ingredients.

7 cups vegetable broth or water
3 tablespoons olive oil
1 medium onion, finely chopped
2 garlic cloves, finely chopped
4 cups bite-size cauliflower florets
$\frac{1}{4}$ cup dark raisins
2 cups arborio rice
$\frac{1}{2}$ teaspoon saffron threads
1 cup dry white wine
$\frac{1}{3}$ cup lightly toasted pine nuts
2 tablespoons unsalted butter
$\frac{1}{2}$ cup freshly grated Parmesan cheese
Salt and freshly ground black pepper, to taste

1. In a saucepan, bring the broth or water to a simmer. Keep the liquid at a bare simmer while you proceed with the risotto.

2. In a heavy 4-quart casserole, heat the olive oil over medium heat. Add the onion and garlic and cook, stirring, for 7 to 8 minutes, until the onion starts to color. Add the cauliflower and raisins and cook, stirring, for 2 minutes. Add the rice and saffron and cook, stirring with a wooden spoon, for about 2 minutes, until the rice is well coated. When the grains become slightly translucent, add the wine and cook, stirring, until the liquid is completely absorbed.

3. Add 1 cup of hot broth or water, and stir frequently, until the liquid is almost absorbed, then continue adding about $\frac{1}{2}$ cup of liquid at a time, stirring until each is almost completely absorbed. Adjust the heat so that the risotto is always at a gentle simmer. After about 18 minutes, the rice should be pleasantly al dente and creamy at the same time.

4. Stir in a final $\frac{1}{4}$ cup of remaining broth. Add pine nuts, butter, and Parmesan and stir to combine with the rice. Season to taste with salt and freshly ground black pepper. Serve risotto as soon as possible, and serve additional Parmesan cheese at the table.

Cauliflower is nothing but a cabbage with a college education. —Mark Twain

Barley "Risotto" with Shiitake Mushrooms

4 servings

In recent years with the resurgence of interest in a large variety of grains, chefs have been coming up with recipes for risotto that substitute other grains for the usual rice. The recipe that follows is based on one I found in a terrific book called **The Splendid Grain,** *by Rebecca Wood. I recommend it to anyone who is interested in learning how to prepare a wider variety of grain dishes.*

One of the advantages of a barley-based risotto is that it can stand for up to an hour without any loss of texture or taste. Simply keep it warm in a very low (200°F) oven.

2 tablespoons extra-virgin olive oil

1 medium onion, finely chopped

4 garlic cloves, finely chopped

1 small celery rib, finely chopped

$\frac{1}{2}$ pound shiitake mushrooms, stems removed, caps thinly sliced

$\frac{1}{4}$ cup minced fresh parsley

2 cups pearl barley (see page 162)

1 vegetarian bouillon cube, dissolved in 2 cups boiling water

5 cups boiling water

$\frac{1}{4}$ cup heavy cream

6 ounces crumbled blue cheese

Salt and freshly ground black pepper, to taste

1. In a heavy 4-quart casserole, heat the olive oil over medium heat. Add the onion, garlic, celery, and mushrooms and cook, stirring, for about 5 minutes, until the mushrooms are tender. Stir in the parsley and the pearl barley and cook, stirring for 2 minutes, until all the grains are coated with oil.

2. Add the vegetable bouillon, reduce heat to low, and cook, stirring occasionally, for about 10 minutes, until the liquid is absorbed. Add half the boiling water and continue to cook, stirring occasionally, for 15 to 20 minutes, until the liquid is absorbed. Add the remaining water and cook, stirring frequently, until all the liquid is absorbed and the barley is cooked through and creamy, about 20 minutes.

3. Stir in the cream and blue cheese. Season to taste with salt and pepper. Serve in shallow soup plates.

> The cultivation of food plants began in Neolithic times, when barley was one of the first to be thus raised deliberately; but we know that it was eaten ever earlier, by prehistoric men who gathered the seeds of the wild grass which was the ancestor of our modern varieties and, before they had learned how to make flour, scattered them over meat and other foods to add a nutty seasoning.—Waverley Root

Vegetarian Paella

This famous dish from Spain is named for the vessel in which it is cooked—a wide, flat-bottomed pan with handles on the sides that can be made of earthenware or metal. You may be surprised to know that the paella most commonly served in this country—a dish consisting of rice, seafood, chicken and sausage—is much less authentic than a dish of paella that is completely vegetarian. The original paella, hailing from Valencia, contained rabbit, chicken, beans, and snails. Paella with seafood came much later, but the ingredients of the two are never combined. Vegetarian paellas, however, are not at all uncommon, and this one never fails to satisfy.

5 cups vegetable stock or water

3 tablespoons extra-virgin olive oil

1 large white or Spanish onion, finely chopped

6 garlic cloves, finely minced

$\frac{1}{2}$ teaspoon hot red pepper flakes

1 large red bell pepper, seeded and diced

1 small fennel bulb, trimmed and cut into $\frac{1}{4}$-inch dice

2 cups Spanish Valencia rice or Italian arborio rice

$\frac{1}{2}$ cup red wine

2 cups chopped fresh or canned (drained) tomatoes

$\frac{1}{4}$ cup finely snipped basil leaves

2 tablespoons fresh minced fennel fronds

1 tablespoon finely chopped fresh oregano, or 1 teaspoon dried oregano

1 teaspoon salt

Freshly ground black pepper, to taste

$\frac{1}{2}$ cup dried chestnuts*, soaked for 1 hour in warm water, drained and coarsely chopped

1 10-ounce package frozen artichoke hearts, thawed and quartered

1 cup fresh or frozen peas, thawed

*Dried chestnuts are available from Goldmine Foods, see mail-order sources, p. 173.

1. In a saucepan, bring the stock or water to a simmer. Keep the liquid at a bare simmer while you proceed with the paella.

2. In a large sauté pan or deep-sided skillet, heat the olive oil over medium heat. Add the onion, garlic, and red pepper flakes and sauté for 2 to 3 minutes, until onions are softened but not colored. Add the bell pepper and fennel and cook, stirring, for 5 minutes. Add the rice and cook, stirring with a wooden spoon, for about 2 minutes, until the rice is well coated. When the grains become slightly translucent, add the wine, tomatoes, basil, fennel, oregano leaves, salt, and pepper. Cook, stirring, for 8 to 10 minutes, until the liquid is completely absorbed.

3. Add half the vegetable stock or water and cook at a gentle simmer, stirring frequently, until most of the liquid has been absorbed. Continue adding vegetable stock or water, $\frac{1}{2}$ cup at a time, and cook, stirring, until the liquid is absorbed, 8 to 10 minutes.

4. Stir in the chestnuts, artichoke hearts, and peas. Remove from heat, cover, and let stand for 5 minutes before serving.

Variation
Substitute 1 cup canned chick-peas, drained and rinsed, for the dried chestnuts.

Stir-fried Wild Rice with Asparagus and Mushrooms

Wild rice is not really a rice, but the seed of a an aquatic grass native to the northern lake country of Minnesota. It is one of the few grains that is native to North America, and it has a superb flavor and texture. In this stir-fry it is blended with the nutty flavors of short-grain brown rice and highlighted by the earthy flavors of shiitake mushrooms and asparagus.

2 tablespoons extra-virgin olive oil

4 large shallots, finely chopped

12 fresh shiitake mushrooms, stems discarded and caps thinly sliced

$\frac{1}{2}$ teaspoon salt

Freshly ground black pepper, to taste

2 tablespoons finely minced fresh parsley

1 tablespoon finely minced fresh dill

1 teaspoon grated lemon zest

1 teaspoon fresh lemon thyme leaves (optional)

$\frac{1}{2}$ cup vegetable broth or water

1 pound asparagus, trimmed, peeled, and cut into 1-inch pieces

$1\frac{1}{2}$ cups steamed wild rice (see page 162)

$1\frac{1}{2}$ cups cooked short-grain brown rice (see page 161)

Gomasio (see page 169), for garnish

1. In a large sauté pan or wok, heat the oil over medium heat. Add the shallots and cook, stirring, for 1 to 2 minutes. Add the mushrooms and sauté, stirring, for 5 minutes.

2. Add the salt, pepper, parsley, dill, lemon zest, lemon thyme leaves, and vegetable broth or water. Add the asparagus, stir, cover the pan, and cook for 3 to 5 minutes, until the asparagus turns bright green.

3. Stir in the wild and brown rice, making sure to mix well. Cook over medium heat, stirring occasionally, until the rice is heated all the way through. I like to cook the

rice until it starts to get crusty on the bottom and stir the crusty bits into the rice. Pass the Gomasio for seasoning at the table.

Wild rice figures prominently in the lore of the Ojibwa, who once lived on the East Coast. Their prophets foretold a great journey that would end in a place where abundant food grew in the water. By the mid-1500s, they migrated to northern Wisconsin and Minnesota and, like the Sioux and Fox who had lived there before them, quickly adopted wild rice as a staple food.—Barbara Grunes and Virginia Van Vynckt, *All-American Waves of Grain*

Vegetable Fried Rice

4 main-dish servings

Don't hesitate to prepare this tasty dish even if you have to start from scratch and cook the rice earlier in the day. The results are worth it—a healthful and delicious one-dish meal.

4 cups cooked and chilled white or brown rice (see pages 160 or 161)

2 tablespoons peanut or canola oil

1 medium onion, halved and thinly sliced

2 to 3 garlic cloves, finely minced

1 teaspoon freshly grated ginger

6 scallions, green parts included, trimmed and chopped, green parts reserved for garnish

1 green or red bell pepper, seeded and chopped

$\frac{1}{4}$ pound fresh mushrooms (your choice), sliced

$1\frac{1}{2}$ cups shredded green cabbage

$1\frac{1}{2}$ cups fresh bean sprouts, rinsed and drained

$\frac{1}{2}$ teaspoon salt

3 tablespoons soy sauce

$\frac{1}{2}$ teaspoon sugar

Freshly ground black pepper

1 cup fresh or frozen (thawed) green peas

2 to 3 teaspoons toasted sesame oil

Additional soy sauce

GARNISH

1 bunch watercress, stems removed, leaves coarsely chopped

1. Crumble the rice with your fingers to separate the grains. Set aside.

2. In a large sauté pan or wok, heat the oil over medium heat. Add the onion and stir-fry for 2 to 3 minutes, until the onion is translucent. Add the garlic, ginger, and white parts of scallions and stir-fry for 30 seconds.

3. Add the pepper and mushrooms and stir-fry for 2 minutes. Add the cabbage, bean sprouts, salt, soy sauce, sugar, and several grindings of black pepper and stir-fry for 2 minutes more. Add the peas and rice, mix well, and stir-fry until everything is hot and all the liquid has been absorbed, 5 to 6 minutes. (If the mixture is too dry while cooking, stir in 2 to 3 tablespoons water.)

4. Remove from heat, stir in the sesame oil, and additional soy sauce, if desired. Garnish with chopped green scallion tops and chopped watercress, if using.

Variations

Select any of the following ingredients to add to your fried rice or replace any other ingredient: cooked corn kernels, shredded carrots, scrambled eggs, cooked broccoli, steamed, chopped greens, toasted peanuts, cashews, pine nuts, pumpkin or sunflower seeds.

Thai Fried Rice with Pineapple

This is a delicious fried rice that sparkles with the flavors of Thai cooking. The pineapple adds a wonderful sweet contrast to the savory dish.

1 ounce large Chinese mushrooms

4 cups cooked and chilled jasmine or basmati rice (see page 160)

3 tablespoons peanut or canola oil

6 garlic cloves, finely chopped

1 medium onion, finely chopped

$\frac{1}{4}$ pound green beans, trimmed and diced

1 large carrot, shredded

3 large eggs, whisked together with a fork

3 tablespoons soy sauce

2 tablespoons Asian fish sauce

2 cups finely chopped fresh or canned pineapple

Freshly ground black pepper, to taste

$\frac{1}{2}$ cup fresh cilantro leaves

4 scallions, thinly sliced

2 limes, quartered

2 or 3 finely chopped fresh, green or red chilies (**optional**)

1. Soak the mushrooms in warm water for 20 minutes, until they are soft and plump. Remove and discard the stalks and cut the mushroom caps into small dice.

2. Crumble the rice with your fingers to separate the grains. Set aside.

3. In a large sauté pan or wok, heat 2 tablespoons of the oil over high heat until almost smoking. Add the mushrooms, garlic, onion, and green beans and stir-fry for 1 minute.

4. Add the remaining tablespoon of oil and let heat for 30 seconds. Stir in the rice and carrots and stir-fry for 2 minutes. Add the eggs, soy sauce and fish sauce and

stir-fry for 5 minutes over high heat. Stir in the pineapple and stir-fry for 1 minute. Season to taste with the pepper.

5. Spoon the rice onto plates and garnish with cilantro leaves and scallions. Place 2 lime wedges on each plate so that each person can squeeze lime juice on the rice as they eat. Pass a small bowl of chilies to sprinkle on the rice if you and your guests like to heat things up a bit.

Fish Sauce

Thai fish sauce (nam pla) or Vietnamese fish sauce (nuoc mam) can be found in Asian grocery stores or by mail. See mail-order sources, p. 173.

Fried Rice with Broccoli, Peas, and Sun-dried Tomatoes

4 main-course servings

A great fried rice dish with good-for-you broccoli and splashes of flavor and color from sun-dried tomatoes.

1 bunch broccoli (about $\frac{1}{2}$ pound)

4 cups cooked and chilled white or brown rice (see page 160 or 161)

3 large eggs

$\frac{1}{2}$ teaspoon salt

$\frac{1}{4}$ teaspoon white pepper

2 tablespoons peanut or canola oil

6 garlic cloves, finely minced

1 teaspoon finely minced ginger

1 cup fresh or frozen peas (thawed)

2 tablespoons water

1 tablespoon soy sauce

1 teaspoon dark roasted sesame oil

1 teaspoon sugar

$\frac{1}{4}$ cup sun-dried tomatoes, cut into thin strips

3 scallions, trimmed and finely sliced

$\frac{1}{4}$ cup finely minced fresh cilantro

1. Trim the broccoli and separate the heads into small florets. Peel the stalks and cut them into $\frac{1}{4}$-inch dice. Set aside.

2. Crumble the rice with your fingers to separate the grains. Set aside.

3. In a small bowl, beat the eggs together with the salt and white pepper. Set aside.

4. Heat a wok or sauté pan over high heat for 30 seconds. Add the oil and swirl it around. Add the garlic and ginger and stir-fry for 30 seconds. Add the broccoli and

peas and stir-fry for 1 minute. Add the water, soy sauce, sesame oil, and sugar. Continue to stir-fry for 2 to 3 minutes, until the broccoli is cooked.

5. Add the rice and sun-dried tomatoes and stir-fry for 3 minutes more. Add the eggs and stir-fry for another 2 minutes. Stir in scallions and cilantro, remove from heat, and serve.

Basic Congee with Five Variations

Like chicken soup in the west, congee is an Asian cure for what ails you. Coming down with a cold? Have a tummy ache? Paying the piper after a night of indulgence? Or just feeling a little blue? Congee, a thick gruel made by boiling rice in a large amount of water, is just the thing to fix you up and make the world come right. Congee is also a popular breakfast dish, probably because it is so kind to your whole system.

If you have a slow cooker tucked away somewhere, pull it out—it's perfect for making congee. Feel free to substitute white rice for the brown rice if you prefer.

$\frac{1}{2}$ cup short-grain brown rice (see page 161)
$\frac{1}{2}$ cup glutinous brown rice
8 cups water
Salt to taste

TOPPINGS

salt
freshly ground black pepper
ghee or butter
roasted sesame oil
finely sliced scallions
finely minced fresh cilantro
grated fresh gingerroot
soy sauce
hot chili sauce

1. Place the rice and water in a heavy 4-quart pot or Dutch oven. Bring to a boil, reduce the heat to very low (use a flame tamer if you have one), cover, leaving the lid slightly ajar, and simmer for $1\frac{1}{2}$ to 2 hours, stirring the rice every 30 minutes with a wooden spoon, until the rice has thickened to a porridgelike consistency.

2. Add salt to taste and serve with any of the toppings listed above.

Variations

- Prepare the basic congee. Prepare 1 head of romaine lettuce or 1 head of bok choy by separating the leaves, washing them, and cutting into $\frac{1}{2}$-inch strips. When the congee is almost ready, stir in the lettuce or bok choy strips together with 3 finely sliced scallions, 1 tablespoon soy sauce, and one $\frac{1}{2}$-inch-thick slice fresh ginger. Return to a boil, reduce heat to a simmer, and cook, covered, for 3 minutes longer.

- For an Indian-style congee, prepare the basic recipe. When the congee is done, add salt and lots of freshly ground black pepper. Heat 3 tablespoons ghee or butter in a small skillet, add 2 tablespoons whole cumin seeds, and cook for 1 minute. Pour the cumin-flavored butter over the congee, mix well, and serve.

- Prepare the basic congee. When the congee is cooked, stir in 1 beaten egg, 1 tablespoon finely minced ginger, 3 thinly sliced scallions, $\frac{1}{2}$ pound spinach (trimmed, washed, and dried), and 1 chopped, large, ripe tomato. Cook for 3 minutes longer, until the spinach is wilted and the tomato is heated through. Season with salt and freshly ground black pepper to taste and serve.

- Prepare the basic congee. When the congee is cooked, heat up any prepared leftover vegetables and stir them in. Season to taste with salt and freshly ground black pepper and serve.

- For a sweet congee, prepare the basic recipe and when it is cooked, add butter, sugar, honey, or maple syrup to taste, and a little bit of heavy cream.

Gratins
and Casseroles

Potato, Onion, and Tomato Gratin

This recipe is adapted from one that appears in Chez Panisse Vegetables, *by the great Alice Waters. I love it because it is so simple and combines two of my favorite foods—tomatoes and potatoes. With some good bread and a salad it makes a wonderful meal, particularly on a summer evening, outdoors.*

1 medium onion, cut in half and thinly sliced

Salt and freshly ground black pepper, to taste

$2\frac{1}{2}$ pounds Yellow Finn or red potatoes, peeled and cut into $\frac{1}{8}$ inch slices (keep them in a bowl of cold water until needed)

1 tablespoon fresh thyme leaves, or 1 teaspoon dried thyme

$1\frac{1}{2}$ pounds ripe tomatoes, cored and cut into thin slices

4 garlic cloves, very thinly sliced

2 tablespoons extra-virgin olive oil

$\frac{1}{2}$ cup white wine

1 cup vegetable broth

1 tablespoon unsalted butter (optional)

1. Preheat the oven to 375°F. Lightly oil a 9-inch square or oval gratin dish with 2-inch sides.

2. Lay the onion slices on the bottom of the dish. Sprinkle with salt and pepper. Arrange half the potatoes over the onions and sprinkle with salt and pepper and half the thyme. Arrange all the tomato slices over the potatoes and cover with the garlic slices. Sprinkle with salt, pepper, and remaining thyme. Add a layer of the remaining potatoes, seasoned with salt and pepper.

3. Drizzle the olive oil all over the casserole. Pour in the white wine and enough vegetable broth to come two thirds of the way up the sides of the dish. Dot with butter, if using.

4. Cover with foil and bake for 45 minutes. Remove the foil and press down on the potatoes to make sure they are adequately moistened. Bake for another 40 minutes, or until the top is golden brown and a knife pierces through to the bottom very easily. Serve with French bread and a green salad.

The first Europeans to see the potato, probably near Quito, Ecuador, not much later than 1530, were Pizarro's men, one of whom, Pedro de Cienza de Leon, wrote about it in his *Chronicle of Peru*, of which the first part was published in 1553. South American Indians must have been cultivating the potato long before the discovery of America.—Waverley Root, *Food*

Casserole of Lentils, Rice, and Chili Peppers

Together, lentils and rice form a perfect protein, rich in vitamins, minerals, and fiber. Serve this tasty casserole with a green salad and some good bread.

$\frac{2}{3}$ cup short-grain brown rice (see page 161), soaked in cold water for 1 hour and drained

1 cup lentils, picked over and rinsed

4 ounces grated Monterey Jack cheese

1 medium onion, finely chopped

1 4-ounce can New Mexican green chilies, drained and chopped

1 cup canned whole Italian tomatoes, drained and chopped

2 garlic cloves, finely chopped

$\frac{1}{2}$ teaspoon salt

$\frac{1}{2}$ teaspoon dried oregano

$\frac{1}{2}$ teaspoon dried thyme

$\frac{1}{4}$ to $\frac{1}{2}$ teaspoon red pepper flakes

Freshly ground black pepper, to taste

3 cups vegetable broth

$\frac{1}{2}$ cup dry white wine

1. Preheat the oven to 350°F.

2. Combine the rice, lentils, half the cheese, onion, green chilies, tomatoes, garlic, salt, oregano, thyme, red pepper flakes, and freshly ground black pepper in a bowl and mix well.

3. Transfer the mixture to an ungreased, ovenproof $1\frac{1}{2}$-quart casserole. Combine the vegetable broth and white wine and pour over the casserole ingredients. Bake for 1 hour and 15 minutes, stirring twice during the baking, until the rice and lentils are cooked through. Sprinkle the remaining cheese over the casserole and continue baking for another 10 or 15 minutes, until the cheese melts and bubbles.

Tian of Rice and Zucchini

Tian is the name for the Provençal earthenware baking dish in which this casse-role is baked. This is a lovely meal to make in summer, when the herbs and veg-etables are at their prime. It's great at lunch, for a light supper, or cut up in small squares and served as an hors d'oeuvre.

2 tablespoons extra-virgin olive oil

1 medium onion, finely chopped

2 pounds zucchini (6 to 8 small ones), cut into very small dice

2 ripe tomatoes, cut into small dice

3 garlic cloves, finely chopped

$\frac{1}{2}$ teaspoon salt

Freshly ground black pepper, to taste

4 eggs, lightly beaten

$\frac{1}{2}$ cup grated Gruyère cheese

2 tablespoons freshly grated Parmesan cheese

$\frac{1}{2}$ cup finely chopped fresh parsley

$\frac{1}{2}$ cup shredded basil leaves

$\frac{1}{2}$ teaspoon fresh thyme leaves

$\frac{1}{2}$ cup cooked white or brown rice (see pages 160 or 161)

1. Preheat the oven to 375°F. Oil or butter the insides of a gratin or baking dish.

2. In a large skillet, heat the oil over medium heat. Add the onion and sauté for 3 to 5 minutes, until the onion is wilted. Lower the heat, add the zucchini, tomatoes, and garlic and sauté, stirring frequently, for about 10 minutes, until the zucchini has softened. Remove from heat and season with salt and pepper to taste.

3. In a large bowl, beat the eggs together with both cheeses. Stir in the cooked zucchini mixture, the parsley, basil, and thyme leaves. Stir in the cooked rice. Transfer to the prepared gratin or casserole. Bake for 40 to 45 minutes, until firm and golden on top. Remove from the oven.

4. The tian can be served hot, warm, or at room temperature. It can be cooled, covered with plastic wrap, and kept in the refrigerator for 1 day.

Barley with Spinach and Peas

Barley, the oldest cultivated grain, is grown all over the world, in climates as varied as the Arctic Circle and the tropics. Although we are most familiar with barley as an ingredient in soup, it is an excellent grain for a vegetarian main course. It is high in protein and soluble fiber, as well as a powerhouse of vitamins and minerals. It is also extremely satisfying and delicious.

2 tablespoons extra-virgin olive oil

1 large onion, finely chopped

3 carrots, diced

2 celery ribs, finely chopped

4 cups vegetable broth or water

$1\frac{1}{2}$ cups pearl barley (see page 162), well rinsed

$\frac{1}{2}$ teaspoon salt, less if the broth is salty

1 pound fresh spinach, washed, stems removed, torn into bite-size pieces, or 1
   10-ounce package chopped frozen spinach, thawed

$1\frac{1}{2}$ cups fresh or frozen peas

1 tablespoon unsalted butter (optional)

$\frac{1}{2}$ cup freshly grated Parmesan cheese

Freshly ground black pepper, to taste

1. In a 4-quart casserole or Dutch oven, heat the olive oil over medium heat. Add the onion and cook, stirring, for 5 minutes, until softened. Add the carrots and celery and cook, stirring frequently, for another 5 minutes.

2. Add the vegetable broth or water and bring to a boil. Stir in the barley and salt, reduce heat to a simmer, and cook, covered, for 30 minutes. Stir in the spinach and peas, cover, and cook for another 15 minutes.

3. Remove from heat and let stand, covered, for 5 to 10 minutes. Stir in the butter and Parmesan cheese. Season with freshly ground black pepper to taste and serve.

American farmers grow plenty of barley—about seven million acres annually. But very little of it shows up as itself in the grocery store. More than half goes into animal feed; another 30 percent or so is malted, to be used in brewing and as a sweetener and flavoring in breakfast cereals and other foods.—Barbara Grunes and Virginia Van Vynckt, *All-American Waves of Grain*

Barley, Brown Rice, and Lentil Casserole

Here's an easy one-dish, one-pot casserole that practically makes itself. Rich in complex carbohydrates and fiber, this is the kind of meal that helps keep us healthy.

2 tablespoons olive or canola oil

1 large onion, finely chopped

4 garlic cloves, finely minced

$\frac{1}{2}$ cup (1 4-ounce can) chopped New Mexican green chilies

$\frac{1}{4}$ cup shredded basil leaves

1 tablespoon fresh chopped oregano, or 1 teaspoon dried oregano

1 tablespoon fresh thyme leaves, or 1 teaspoon dried thyme

1 cup pearl barley (see page 162)

$\frac{1}{2}$ cup long-grain brown rice (see page 161)

1 cup French lentils* or brown lentils, picked over to remove debris and rinsed

$3\frac{1}{2}$ cups vegetable broth or water

$\frac{1}{2}$ cup white wine

1 teaspoon salt or more to taste

Freshly ground black pepper, to taste

4 ounces shredded Monterey Jack or crumbled feta cheese

1. Preheat the oven to 350°F.

2. In a heavy 3-quart casserole, heat the oil over medium heat. Add onion and garlic and sauté for about 3 minutes, stirring frequently, until the onion has wilted. Stir in the chilies, basil, oregano, and thyme. Add the barley and rice, stirring until each grain is coated with oil. Add the lentils, broth, wine, salt, pepper, and half the cheese. Stir well, cover the pot, and bake for $1\frac{1}{2}$ hours. Stir the pot halfway through the baking.

3. Uncover the pot, sprinkle the top with remaining cheese, and bake for another 5 to 10 minutes, until the cheese melts and bubbles.

*Lentilles du Puy

Stews,
Sautés, Chili,
and Curry

Ragout of Potatoes, Leeks, Asparagus, and Mushrooms

I love stews, ragouts, and fricassees. But I have always been one of those people who prefer the sauce and the vegetables to the meat. I started leaving the meat out of my stews several years ago when I found the original version of this recipe in Gourmet *magazine (April 1995). I have made it with many variations over the years—substituting frozen baby lima beans for the peas, morels or chanterelles for the shiitakes, fiddlehead ferns for the asparagus—and it remains a favorite in every incarnation.*

4 tablespoons extra-virgin olive oil

1 pound Yukon Gold or fingerling potatoes, scrubbed and cut into $\frac{1}{2}$-inch dice

Salt, to taste

2 large leeks, white and pale green parts only, washed and cut crosswise into $\frac{1}{2}$-inch slices

1 pound asparagus, trimmed and cut into 1-inch pieces

$\frac{1}{2}$ pound shiitake mushrooms, stems removed and caps quartered

1 cup fresh or frozen green peas

1 cup vegetable broth

$\frac{1}{2}$ cup dry white wine

Freshly ground black pepper, to taste

$\frac{1}{4}$ cup finely chopped fresh parsley

2 tablespoons snipped chives

1. In a large sauté pan or wok, heat 2 tablespoons olive oil over high heat. Add the potatoes, sprinkle with salt, and sauté, turning the potatoes over from time to time, for 8 minutes, until they are golden. Remove the potatoes and reserve.

2. Heat 1 tablespoon of the remaining olive oil in the same pan, over medium heat, and add the leeks. Sauté for 2 or 3 minutes, stirring frequently, until lightly browned. Remove the leeks and reserve.

3. Heat the final tablespoon of olive oil in the same pan, over high heat. Add the asparagus, sprinkle with salt, and sauté, stirring frequently, for 2 minutes. Add the mushrooms and sauté, stirring frequently for another 2 minutes.

4. Add the vegetable broth and wine and bring to a boil. Add the reserved potatoes, leeks, and peas. Reduce heat to a simmer and cook for 5 to 8 minutes, until the potatoes are tender. Season to taste with salt and freshly ground black pepper. Garnish with parsley and chives and serve.

Variations
- Roast a head of garlic in the oven and cool (see page 171). Squeeze out the roasted garlic paste and stir into the ragout at the very end.
- Stir in $\frac{1}{4}$ cup heavy cream when the ragout is almost done. Reheat and serve.

Caribbean Vegetable Stew

This is a great stew, hearty and satisfying, with an unusual combination of vegetables. I make it all winter long, with ingredients purchased easily from a supermarket. I don't know why it's called a Caribbean stew—perhaps because it is so warming that it makes me feel as if I've gone there.

2 tablespoons canola oil

2 large onions, coarsely chopped

6 garlic cloves, finely chopped

$\frac{1}{2}$ pound (about 3 cups) shredded white cabbage

$\frac{1}{2}$ cup dry white wine

1 serrano or jalapeño chili, finely chopped

$\frac{1}{4}$ teaspoon hot red pepper flakes

1 tablespoon grated fresh ginger

2 cups vegetable broth or water

1 pound (about 3) sweet potatoes, peeled and cut into $\frac{1}{2}$-inch cubes

2 cups chopped fresh or canned tomatoes

2 cups sliced fresh or frozen okra

1 teaspoon salt

Freshly ground black pepper, to taste

3 tablespoons fresh lime juice

$\frac{1}{4}$ cup chopped fresh cilantro

$\frac{1}{2}$ cup chopped dry roasted peanuts

1. Heat the oil in 4-quart casserole or Dutch oven over medium heat. Add the onions and garlic and sauté, stirring frequently, for 2 to 3 minutes. Add the cabbage, wine, serrano or jalapeño chili, red pepper flakes, and ginger. Continue to sauté, stirring frequently, for 10 minutes.

2. Add the vegetable broth or water and sweet potatoes. Bring the stew to a boil, reduce heat to a simmer, and cook, partially covered, for 10 minutes.

3. Add the tomatoes, okra, salt, several grindings of black pepper, and lime juice. Simmer the stew for an additional 15 to 20 minutes, until all the vegetables are tender.

4. Taste for seasoning and stir in the cilantro. Top each serving with a sprinkling of chopped peanuts.

I would like to find a stew that will give me heartburn immediately, instead of at three o'clock in the morning.—John Barrymore

Tofu in Red Chili Sauce

6 to 8 servings

In this recipe, adapted from one I found in a book called Hot and Spicy and Meatless, *the tofu replaces the meat to make a delicious and unusual vegetarian stew. Serve with tortillas or corn bread and a green salad.*

4 pounds (4 packages) firm tofu

$\frac{1}{4}$ cup olive oil

1 large onion, coarsely chopped

4 large garlic cloves, coarsely chopped

$\frac{1}{4}$ cup mild New Mexico chili powder

1 chile chipotle in adobo sauce, finely diced

1 teaspoon ground coriander

1 teaspoon Mexican oregano, pulverized between your fingers

1 teaspoon toasted, ground cumin (see page 172)

1 tablespoon honey

2 tablespoons balsamic vinegar

2 tablespoons tamari soy sauce

$\frac{1}{4}$ cup roasted pumpkin seeds

2 cups vegetable stock

1. Slice the block of tofu lengthwise and place them between layers of paper towels. Place large books, heavy pots, or any other weighty object of your choice on the tofu to press out the excess liquid. Let the weighted tofu sit for 15 to 20 minutes.

2. Slice the tofu into $\frac{1}{2}$-inch cubes. Heat the olive oil in a large, heavy skillet over medium-high heat until it is hot but not smoking. Add the tofu cubes and sauté until the tofu is golden brown. Remove with a slotted spoon and drain on paper towels. Place the tofu in a glass or ceramic bowl and set aside.

3. Remove all but 1 tablespoon of the olive oil from the skillet. Add the onion and garlic and sauté over medium-high heat for about 5 minutes, until the onion has softened. Lower the heat, add the chili powder and the diced chile chipotle, and cook,

stirring, for 5 minutes longer. Stir in coriander, oregano, cumin, honey, vinegar, and soy sauce. Cook, stirring, for 1 minute and remove from heat.

4. Place the pumpkin seeds in the bowl of a food processor or blender and process until they are pulverized. Add 1 cup of stock and process to blend. Add onion-chili mixture from the skillet and process to blend.

5. Place the mixture in a large saucepan, add the remaining stock, and heat through. Gently stir in the tofu cubes, remove from heat, and let the tofu marinate at room temperature for 1 to 2 hours.

6. Bring the marinating tofu to a boil, reduce heat to low, and simmer, partially covered, for 1 hour.

7. Serve over white or brown cooked rice.

Chile peppers are the biggest food craze to hit the American palate since . . . well, since chocolate. True, garlic and barbecue have had their moments, and even their newsletters, but nothing like the spate of cookbooks, press hype, mail-order purveyors, posters, Christmas lights, and other collectibles that have followed in the wake of chile mania.—John Thorne, *CookBook*

Spicy Squash Stew

Serve this delicious stew over white or brown rice or over polenta (see page 164). I have also served it over baked potatoes or yams that have been split open and seasoned with salt and pepper.

1½ teaspoons cumin seeds

2 teaspoons dried oregano

¼ sesame seeds

¾ cup pumpkin seeds

2 tablespoons canola oil

2 large onions, finely chopped

6 large garlic cloves, finely minced

1 or 2 serrano or jalapeño chilies, seeded and deveined, finely minced

2 to 4 tablespoons New Mexican chili powder

2 pounds butternut or other winter squash, peeled, seeded, and cut into 1-inch cubes

1 28-ounce can whole tomatoes, drained and coarsely chopped

2 cups canned chick-peas, drained and rinsed

3 to 4 cups vegetable stock or water

1 teaspoon salt

Freshly ground black pepper, to taste

1½ cups frozen corn kernels, thawed

½ cup finely chopped cilantro

1. Place a heavy skillet over medium heat, add the cumin seeds, and toast, shaking the skillet occasionally until seeds are hot and have a strong aroma. Remove to a small bowl. Add the oregano and toast for about 5 seconds; remove to the same bowl.

2. In the same pan, toast the sesame seeds until they just start to color and remove. Toast the pumpkin seeds until they start to color and remove.

3. Grind the cumin and oregano in a mortar to a fine powder and reserve. Grind the sesame seeds and pumpkin seeds in a food processor to make a fine meal, and reserve.

4. Heat the oil in a large sauté pan or skillet over medium heat. Add the onion and sauté, stirring, for about 5 minutes, until it softens. Add the garlic, chilies, the reserved powdered cumin and oregano, and 2 tablespoons chili powder. Sauté, stirring, for 2 minutes.

5. Add the squash, tomatoes, chick-peas, 3 cups of vegetable stock or water, salt, and freshly ground black pepper to taste. Simmer the stew for about 20 minutes, adding more stock or water if necessary, until the squash is fork tender.

6. Taste for seasoning and add additional chili powder if desired. Stir in the pumpkin seed and sesame meal and the corn kernels. Simmer for another 5 minutes. Garnish with cilantro and serve.

Squashes and pumpkins were extraordinarily useful and versatile in pre-Colombian America; not only was their flesh eaten as a vegetable, but their blossoms, *flores de cabeza* in Spanish, were cooked and eaten as a great delicacy, as they are still today in Mexico. Their seeds, a rich source of oil and protein, were toasted and eaten out of hand or ground into pastes and thickeners for sauces. And the shells of some varieties were used as bottles, containers, ladles and spoons. It's not every plant that can provide, in one handy package, the food, the bowl to put it in, and the spoon to eat it with!—Elisabeth Rozin, *Blue Corn and Chocolate*

Moroccan Eggplant, Tomato, and Chick-pea Stew

This colorful stew should be served over couscous (see page 163) or quinoa (see page 163). If you know your guests like their food hot and spicy, pass a bowl of harissa (a North African pepper sauce) at the table. You can buy harissa in middle Eastern markets or make your own (see page 167). Pass a basket of warmed pita breads to soak up the stew.

3 tablespoons extra-virgin olive oil

2 large onions, finely chopped

6 garlic cloves, finely chopped

2 cups canned Italian plum tomatoes, drained and coarsely chopped

1 teaspoon paprika

$\frac{1}{2}$ teaspoon ground ginger

$\frac{1}{2}$ teaspoon ground cinnamon

$\frac{1}{4}$ to $\frac{1}{2}$ teaspoon cayenne

$\frac{1}{4}$ teaspoon saffron threads

1 eggplant ($1\frac{1}{2}$ pounds), peeled and cut into $\frac{1}{2}$-inch cubes

3 carrots, peeled and thinly sliced

2 cups canned chick-peas, rinsed and drained

1 cup green olives, pitted

$\frac{1}{2}$ cup whole, blanched almonds

$\frac{1}{3}$ cup dark raisins

$\frac{1}{2}$ lemon, very thinly sliced and pitted

Salt, to taste

Freshly ground black pepper, to taste

$\frac{1}{2}$ cup finely chopped parsley

1. Heat the olive oil in a large sauté pan or casserole over medium heat. Add the onion and garlic and sauté for about 5 minutes, until the onion has wilted.

2. Add the tomatoes, paprika, ginger, cinnamon, cayenne, and saffron threads. Add 1 cup of water, the eggplant, carrots, chick-peas, olives, almonds, raisins, and lemon slices. Bring to a boil, reduce heat to low, and simmer the stew for 30 minutes, until the eggplant and carrots are completely cooked.

3. Season the stew with salt and freshly ground black pepper to taste. Garnish with parsley and serve.

Variations

You can add any number of other vegetables to this stew. Consider green beans, zucchini, sweet potatoes, and red bell peppers. You should limit yourself to the vegetables grown in the Mediterranean region.

Sauté of Summer Vegetables with Corn

Here a quick, easy, and delicious dish for late summer. I like to serve the vegetables in pasta bowls, along with some bread and a plate of sliced tomatoes and sweet onions.

2 tablespoons olive oil

1 large onion, finely chopped

2 garlic cloves, finely chopped

1 or 2 jalapeño peppers (ripened red if possible), seeded and sliced into thin strips

4 large ripe tomatoes, coarsely chopped

2 cups fresh or frozen baby lima beans

6 small zucchini, cut into $\frac{1}{2}$-inch dice

3 cups fresh corn kernels (cut from about 6 ears of corn)

$\frac{1}{4}$ cup shredded basil leaves

$\frac{1}{4}$ cup finely chopped parsley

Salt, to taste

Freshly ground black pepper, to taste

1. In a large sauté pan, heat the oil over medium heat. Add the onion and cook, stirring, for 5 minutes, until the onion has softened. Add the garlic and peppers and sauté, stirring, 2 minutes longer.

2. Add the tomatoes, lima beans, and zucchini. Cook over medium heat, stirring frequently, for 15 minutes. Add the corn kernels, basil, parsley, salt, and pepper and cook for 5 minutes longer. Serve hot or at room temperature.

Andy Weil's Vegetarian Chili

6 servings

Dr. Andrew Weil is well known for many of his achievements in the fields of medical research and practice of alternative medicine and treatments. He is perhaps less well known for his talents as a marvelous and innovative vegetarian cook. I have been lucky enough to be a guest at his dinner table a number of times when he was living in my part of the world, and even years later those meals remain vivid and inspiring in my memory.

1 pound (2 cups) Anasazi beans

4 tablespoons olive oil

2 large onions, sliced into half rounds

1 tablespoon mild red New Mexican chili powder

1 canned chile chipotle in adobo sauce, finely chopped

1 tablespoon Mexican oregano

1 tablespoon roasted, ground cumin (see page 172)

$\frac{1}{2}$ teaspoon ground allspice

1 teaspoon salt

1 28-ounce can crushed tomatoes

3 large carrots, scraped and sliced into rounds

8 ounces fresh shiitake or porcini mushrooms, thinly sliced (optional)

5 large garlic cloves, mashed through a garlic press

A dash or two of balsamic vinegar, or more to taste

Tabasco sauce, to taste

GARNISHES

chopped raw onion

grated Monterey Jack or Cheddar cheese

coarsely chopped fresh tomatoes

shredded romaine lettuce

finely chopped cilantro

fresh lime wedges

1. Pick over the beans to remove any foreign objects. Wash the beans and soak them in water for at least 4 hours, or overnight, changing the water several times.

2. Drain the beans and place them in a large pot with enough water to cover the beans by 2 inches. Bring the beans to a boil, lower the heat, partially cover the pot, and simmer for 2 hours. Stir the beans from time to time and make sure that the level of water remains 2 inches above the surface of the beans.

3. In the meantime, heat 3 tablespoons of the olive oil in a large skillet over medium heat. Add the onions and sauté for about 10 minutes, until they turn golden. Add the chili powder, chile, chipotle, oregano, cumin, allspice, and salt. Cook, stirring, for 2 minutes and add the tomatoes. Simmer for 5 minutes, then add this mixture to the beans, along with the carrots, mushrooms, and garlic. Simmer over low heat for about 1 hour, until the beans become creamy and start to melt into the liquid.

4. Correct the seasonings, adding more chili powder if you want a hotter flavor. Add balsamic vinegar and Tabasco sauce to taste. Serve in bowls accompanied by your choice of garnishes or toppings.

Chili is not so much a food as a state of mind. Addictions to it are formed early in life and the victims never recover. On blue days in October I get this passionate yearning for a bowl of chili, and I nearly lose my mind. . . .—Margaret Cousins

Bean and Corn Chili

6 to 8 servings

This recipe calls for dried beans and a particularly delicious dried corn called chicos. Although this recipe is completely fat free, it is full of flavor and very satisfying. Served bedded in baked acorn squash halves and topped with salsa, it makes a very healthy, colorful dish.

1 pound red kidney beans, or any other red or pinkish beans

1 cup chicos or sweet dried corn

2 dried ancho chilies, stems and seeds removed

1 dried pasilla chili, stems and seeds removed

2 large onions, coarsely chopped

6 large garlic cloves, smashed, peeled, and coarsely chopped

1 tablespoon light brown sugar

2 teaspoons toasted, ground cumin (see page 172)

1 teaspoon Mexican oregano

2 cups chopped, drained, canned tomatoes

1 to 2 teaspoons salt

8 roasted acorn squash halves (see page 166)

$\frac{1}{2}$ cup finely chopped fresh cilantro

Shredded Monterey Jack cheese (optional)

Sour cream (optional)

1. Pick over the beans to remove any foreign objects. Wash the beans and soak them in water for at least 6 hours, or overnight, changing the water several times.

2. Rinse the chicos in several changes of cold water and soak them overnight in 4 cups of water in a large heavy pot in which you will cook the chili.

3. On the following day, cover the chilies with hot water and let them soak for 10 minutes. Purée the chilies with $\frac{1}{2}$ cup of the soaking water in a blender to a smooth paste.

4. Drain the beans and add them to the chicos. Add the puréed chiles, onions, garlic, brown sugar, cumin, and oregano. Add enough water (if necessary) to just cover the beans. Bring to a boil, reduce heat to a simmer, and cook, partially covered, for about 2 hours, until the beans and chicos are tender. Stir the beans from time to time and make sure that there is enough liquid. Add the salt during the last half hour of cooking time.

5. Serve the chili inside a roasted acorn squash. Garnish with chopped cilantro and serve with shredded Monterey Jack and sour cream on the side.

Variations

As a substitute for chicos, use 2 cups of fresh or frozen corn kernels. You can make this a double corn chili by adding 1 10-ounce package of frozen corn kernels to the above recipe. Add to the chili during the last half hour of cooking.

You can also substitute 1 cup of dried posole, soaked overnight, in place of the chicos.

Never heard of chicos?

Chicos, also known as *chicos de horno*, are sweet corn kernels that have been dried without the lime treatment that posole receives. These dried sweet corn kernels have a much more intense corn flavor and chewier texture than fresh corn. It is very popular in the Southwest and among the Pennsylvania Dutch.

In New Mexico and Arizona, dried corn (chicos) added to the chili pot will absorb excess liquid and at the same time give chili a distinctive regional overtone. Fresh corn, scraped from the cob, also brings a wonderful flavor to chili, but doesn't absorb as much liquid as dried corn.—Bill Bridges, *The Great Chili Book*

Native Americans ate corn and beans together at almost every meal and planted them together in the same hill of earth, emphasizing the intimate culinary and nutritional relationship they have always shared.—Elizabeth Rozin, *Blue Corn and Chocolate*

Black Bean Confetti Chili

This chili is based on a favorite black bean salad that always enlivens a buffet table with its colorful accents of red and yellow. Translated into a chili it works extremely well. The addition of chocolate may sound strange, but it actually gives this vegetarian chili a rich depth of flavor that will make even the most ardent carnivore forget about meat. The bulgur provides a background texture similar to ground beef.

2 tablespoons olive oil

2 large onions, coarsely chopped

6 garlic cloves, finely minced or pushed through a garlic press

2 large red bell peppers, cored, seeded, and coarsely chopped

1 large yellow bell pepper, cored, seeded, and coarsely chopped

1 fresh jalapeño chile, cored, seeded, and finely minced

2 tablespoons ancho chili powder

2 tablespoons mild New Mexico chili powder

1 tablespoon toasted, ground cumin (see page 172)

4 cups vegetable stock or water

$\frac{1}{2}$ cup bulgur

1 ounce (1 square) unsweetened chocolate, grated

1 28-ounce can tomatoes, drained and coarsely chopped

8 cups cooked black beans (see page 168), or 4 15-oz cans, rinsed and drained

2 cups fresh corn kernels, or 1 10-ounce package frozen corn kernels, thawed

1 medium red onion, chopped

1. Heat the oil in a large heavy pot over medium heat. Add the onions and garlic and cook, stirring for a few minutes, until the onions have wilted. Add the bell peppers, jalapeño, chili powders, and cumin and cook, stirring, for 3 to 5 minutes longer, until the peppers have softened.

2. Add the vegetable stock or water, bulgur, grated chocolate, tomatoes, and beans. Bring to a boil, lower heat, and simmer gently for 25 minutes. Add the corn kernels, stir, and cook 5 minutes longer.

3. Serve with chopped red onion for garnish.

It is beneficial to one's health not to be carnivorous. The strongest animals, such as the bull, are vegetarians. Look at me. I have ten times as much good health and energy as a meat-eater.—George Bernard Shaw

Vegetarians have wicked, shifty eyes, and laugh in a cold calculating manner. They pinch little children, steal stamps, drink water, favor beards.—J. B. Morton

Chili con Tempeh

Although tempeh is a fairly new ingredient in our culture, it is an ancient food in Indonesia. It is made from hulled soybeans, fermented by a mold that imparts a distinctive flavor and texture. It is very high in protein and vitamins and very low in fat. Its slightly crunchy and chewy texture makes it a popular substitute for meat. Look for it in the refrigerated section of your health-food store.

Not only is this chili completely virtuous, delicious, and satisfying, but it can be prepared in under half an hour.

2 tablespoons olive oil

8 ounces (1 package) tempeh, cut into 1-inch pieces

1 large onion, coarsely chopped

4 garlic cloves, finely minced

6 large mushroom caps (shiitake, cremini, or cultivated white), thinly sliced

2 tablespoons mild New Mexico chili powder

2 tablespoons ancho chili powder

1 teaspoon toasted, ground cumin (see page 172)

1 cup coarsely chopped canned, drained tomatoes

3 carrots, cut into $\frac{1}{2}$-inch chunks

2 celery ribs, cut into $\frac{1}{2}$-inch chunks

3 cups vegetable broth or water

2 cups cooked red kidney beans, or 1 15-ounce can red kidney beans, drained and rinsed

$\frac{1}{4}$ cup bulgur

Salt, to taste

Cayenne, to taste

1. Heat 1 tablespoon of olive oil in a heavy skillet over medium heat until hot but not smoking. Sauté the tempeh until it is lightly browned on both sides. Remove the tempeh to paper towels and reserve.

2. Heat the remaining oil in a heavy pot and sauté the onion and garlic for 5 minutes, until the onion is softened. Add the sliced mushrooms and sauté for 3 minutes longer. Stir in the chili powders and cumin and sauté for 3 more minutes.

3. Add the tomatoes, carrots, celery, vegetable broth or water, kidney beans, bulgur, and tempeh. Stir the chili and bring it to a boil, reduce heat to a simmer, and cook for 20 to 25 minutes, until the chili has thickened. Taste and adjust the seasonings to your liking. Serve in bowls over brown rice (see page 161).

. . . my feeling about chili is this—along in November, when the first norther strikes, and the skies are gray, along about five o'clock in the afternoon, I get to thinking how good chili would taste for supper. It always lives up to expectations. In fact, you don't even mind the cold November winds.—Mrs. Lyndon B. Johnson

Sag Harbor's Vegetarian Chili

8 to 10 servings

The Provisions Health Food Store and Cafe, in the historic whaling village of Sag Harbor, is also a local center of art and music, and a great place to shop, meet friends, and generally hang out. Their terrific vegetarian chili is always on the menu, and I've enjoyed it for years.

3 cups red kidney beans, soaked for 6 hours or overnight, or 4 15-oz cans red kidney beans, rinsed and drained

3 tablespoons olive oil

3 large onions, coarsely chopped

4 tablespoons minced garlic (about 20 medium cloves)

1 14½-ounce can crushed tomatoes

1 large carrot, diced

1 celery rib, diced

1 large baking potato, peeled, cut into ½-inch cubes, and covered with water

1 large yam, peeled, cut into ½-inch cubes, and covered with water

2 to 4 tablespoons chili powder

2 tablespoons tamari soy sauce

1 bay leaf

2 teaspoons dried oregano

2 teaspoons dried basil

2 teaspoons dried marjoram

2 teaspoons dried thyme

1 teaspoon ground coriander

1 teaspoon ground cumin (see page 172)

Salt and freshly ground black pepper, to taste

1 cup tomato juice

1 cup TVP (textured vegetable protein)*

Tabasco sauce, to taste

*TVP (textured vegetable protein) is a protein extract of soybeans that has been formulated into flakes and dried. It is added to dishes as a protein supplement and a meat replacement. It is extremely nutritious, 70 percent to 90 percent protein, and very low in fat. The flavor is very bland and takes on the taste of the dish in which it is reconstituted.

1. Drain the beans and place them in a large heavy pot. Add enough water to cover by 2 inches and bring to a boil. Lower the heat and simmer for $1\frac{1}{2}$ to 2 hours, until the beans are tender.

2. In a large, heavy pot, heat the olive oil over medium heat. Add the onions and sauté, stirring, for 5 to 10 minutes, until onions are soft. Add the garlic and cook, stirring, for 2 minutes. Add the tomatoes, carrot, celery, potatoes, chili powder, tamari, bay leaf, and all the herbs. Stir well, cover the pot, and cook over medium-low heat for 20 to 25 minutes, until the vegetables are tender.

3. Add the beans, salt, pepper, and a little water if necessary, and cook for 30 minutes longer. Add the tomato juice and TVP. Continue cooking for a few minutes over medium heat. The TVP does not need to cook but to fully absorb the liquid and to soften. The chili is done when the TVP is soft and piping hot. Taste and adjust the seasoning with salt, pepper, and a few dashes of Tabasco sauce. Serve with cornbread on the side.

Do you suffer from yellow fever? Malaria? Kidney failure? Apoplexy? Cancer? Heart Disease? Spring fever? The common cold? Have you been rejected in love? Has a witch put a hex on you? Do you have the seven-year itch? Are your fingers swollen and twisted with arthritis? Do you suffer from one intense headache after another, day after day? Would you like to lose weight? Or perhaps you're reading this in the middle of childbirth and find that, although you've been in labor for hours, the baby still hasn't come?

The cure, my friends, is always the same. Peppers. Peppers. Peppers. Eat them. Breathe them. Rub them on your skin. And like some Biblical sufferer, you'll be able to take up your bed and walk and be whole again.—Susan Hazen-Hammond, *Chile Pepper Fever*

Green Chili with White Beans

This is as far away as chili gets from the traditional meat lover's "bowl of red." It is an elegant, low-fat, vegetarian chili with a hint of mysterious smoky flavor from the chile chipotle. Serve it with brown or white rice and a big green salad, for a low-on-the-food-chain, politically correct, high-complex-carbohydrate meal. This is a great party dish.

4 tablespoons olive oil

6 pounds large yellow onions, peeled and coarsely chopped

6 large carrots, peeled and coarsely chopped

6 celery ribs, trimmed and coarsely chopped

8 garlic cloves, finely chopped or pushed through a garlic press

6 green Poblano, New Mexico, or Anaheim chilies, roasted, peeled, seeded, and finely chopped (see directions pages 169–70), or 2 4-ounce cans chopped mild green chilies

2 to 3 fresh jalapeño peppers, seeded and finely chopped

1 to 2 chiles chipotles in adobo sauce, finely minced (optional)

4 large ripe tomatoes, peeled, seeded, and coarsely chopped, or 1 28-oz can whole tomatoes, drained and coarsely chopped

1 bunch parsley, finely chopped

2 tablespoons whole cumin seeds, toasted

1 tablespoon dried oregano

1 teaspoon dried thyme

4 cups white beans, soaked 4 hours or overnight

3 quarts vegetable broth or water

1 tablespoon freshly ground black pepper (or to taste)

2 bay leaves

Salt, to taste

1 cup finely chopped fresh cilantro

1 tablespoon fresh thyme leaves

1. Heat the olive oil in a large pot over medium heat. Sauté the onions, carrots, and celery for 10 to 15 minutes. Add the garlic and chilies and sauté, stirring for 2 minutes longer. Stir in tomatoes, parsley, cumin, oregano, and thyme.

2. Drain the beans and add them together with $2\frac{1}{2}$ quarts broth or water to the pot with the vegetables. Add black pepper and bay leaves.

3. Simmer, uncovered, over low heat for $2\frac{1}{2}$ to 3 hours until beans are tender and the chili has thickened. Check the chili frequently while it is cooking and add more broth or water if necessary. Season with salt and pepper to taste. Add more chile chipotle if you like it hotter. Stir in chopped cilantro and fresh thyme leaves. Remove bay leaves and serve. Serve with rice, Fresh Tomato Salsa (recipe follows), and a bowl of freshly grated Monterey Jack cheese.

Winter Squash in a Green Curry Sauce

This is a great curry for a cool evening. Use any available winter squash—butternut, banana, Delicata, Hubbard, turban, or even sugar pumpkin. These orange-fleshed beauties are full of beta-carotene, iron, potassium, and fiber. Their slightly sweet flavors marry very well with a spicy curry sauce. Serve with brown or white rice and a salad or steamed greens. The original recipe comes from Real Vegetarian Thai, *by* Nancie McDermott. *This is the kind of book that makes me want to make every recipe in it (and I have). I've altered this one slightly by replacing half of the coconut milk with soy or evaporated milk to reduce some of the fat.*

2 large shallots, peeled and finely chopped

4 garlic cloves, finely chopped

1-inch knob fresh ginger, peeled and finely chopped

2 fresh, green serrano chilies, cut in half lengthwise, seeded and deveined

1 cup chopped cilantro leaves

1 cup canned unsweetened low-fat coconut milk

1 teaspoon curry powder

1 cup evaporated skim milk or soy milk

1 tablespoon palm sugar or brown sugar

1 teaspoon salt

$\frac{1}{2}$ teaspoon freshly ground black pepper

2 pounds butternut or other winter squash, peeled and cut into 1-inch cubes

1. Combine the shallots, garlic, ginger, chilies, and $\frac{3}{4}$ cup of chopped cilantro in the bowl of a large mortar or a blender. Grind the mixture by hand or in the blender, adding up to 3 tablespoons of water, to make a smooth paste. Set aside the remaining cilantro leaves for garnish.

2. In a medium-size saucepan, bring the coconut milk to a boil and cook for 3 to 4 minutes, stirring frequently, until the milk thickens slightly. Reduce heat to a simmer, stir in the green paste and curry powder, and cook, stirring, for about 3 minutes.

Stir in the evaporated skim milk or soy milk, sugar, salt, and pepper. Add the squash, raise the heat and bring to a boil, stirring frequently. Reduce to a simmer and cook, stirring frequently, for about 20 minutes, until the squash is tender.

3. Garnish with remaining chopped cilantro and serve.

How to Peel a Winter Squash

Hard-skinned winter squashes can be the very devil to cut into manageable pieces and peel. I've heard stories of cooks going at them with ice picks or hurling them full force onto stone floors to make the initial break. Among the easiest to peel is a butternut squash. Cut it in half, crosswise where the neck meets the bulb. Use a sharp paring knife to peel the neck. Scoop out the seeds and pulp in the bulb, cut in half or in quarters, and peel with a paring knife. Cube or slice the flesh as desired.

For larger squashes, you may want to use a cleaver and a rubber mallet. Pound the cleaver into the squash with the mallet until you can cut away a chunk of it. Cut away the hard peel with a sharp knife. Don't worry about cutting away some of the flesh. There is usually plenty left.

Eat hot curry, drink hot soup, burn your lips, and remember my dinner. —Burmese saying

Six-Vegetable Curry

4 to 6 servings

This festive vegetable curry is based in part on a recipe for Chettiar Curry found in A World of Curries, *by Dave DeWitt and Arthur Pais. They tell how the Chettiars, a people from Madras, owned large estates in Burma. They learned this curry from the Burmese farmers who worked for them and were too poor to eat anything but vegetable curry. But the curry speaks for itself, and no one eating it today will feel anything but rich feasting on such a dish.*

1 cup yellow split peas, picked over and rinsed

2 cups water

1 large eggplant (about 1 pound)

3 tablespoons canola oil

2 large onions, finely chopped

4 garlic cloves, finely chopped

2 to 4 fresh green chilies, such as serrano or jalapeño, veins and seeds removed, finely chopped

1 tablespoon finely minced fresh ginger

4 fresh curry leaves, or 4 bay leaves

1 teaspoon salt

1 teaspoon palm sugar or brown sugar

1 teaspoon ground cumin (see page 172)

1 teaspoon ground coriander

1 teaspoon paprika

$\frac{1}{2}$ teaspoon ground turmeric

$\frac{1}{2}$ teaspoon freshly ground black pepper

1 tablespoon tamarind concentrate, dissolved in $\frac{1}{4}$ cup water

2 large all-purpose potatoes, peeled and cut into $\frac{1}{2}$-inch cubes

2 large yams or sweet potatoes, peeled and cut into $\frac{1}{2}$-inch cubes

1 daikon radish, peeled and cut into $\frac{1}{2}$-inch cubes

$1\frac{1}{2}$ cups canned plum tomatoes, drained and chopped

$\frac{1}{4}$ pound string beans, cut into 2-inch lengths

3 cups water

44   The One-Dish Vegetarian

1 cup canned unsweetened low-fat coconut milk

$\frac{1}{2}$ cup fresh cilantro leaves

1. Combine split peas and water in a small saucepan, bring to a boil, reduce heat to a simmer, and cook, stirring occasionally, for 30 minutes, until the peas are soft and melting. The mixture should be quite thick. Set aside.

2. While the peas are cooking, peel the eggplant and cut it into $\frac{3}{4}$-inch cubes. Place the cubes in a colander and sprinkle the eggplant cubes lightly with salt. Let stand in the sink or over a plate for 20 to 30 minutes. Squeeze out the moisture and pat dry with paper towels.

3. In a large sauté pan or Dutch oven, heat the oil and add the onions. Cook over medium heat, stirring, for about 5 minutes, until onions soften. Add the garlic, chilies, ginger, and curry or bay leaves. Sauté for 2 minutes. Add the salt, sugar, cumin, coriander, paprika, turmeric, and black pepper. Sauté, stirring, for 1 minute.

4. Stir in the cooked yellow split peas together with their cooking water. Bring the mixture to a simmer, cover the pan, and cook for 2 minutes. Add the tamarind liquid, eggplant, potatoes, sweet potatoes or yams, radish cubes, tomatoes, and string beans. Add the water and coconut milk. Bring to a simmer, cover, and cook for about 20 minutes, until all the vegetables are fork tender. If you have used bay leaves instead of curry leaves, fish them out and discard them before serving.

5. Sprinkle the curry with cilantro leaves and serve over rice.

Variations

- Tamarind pulp has more flavor than the concentrate. To substitute in this recipe, take a walnut-size lump of pulp and soak in $\frac{1}{2}$ cup warm water for 10 to 15 minutes. Strain through a sieve, pressing out as much liquid as possible from the pulp. Discard remaining pulp and add liquid to the recipe.
- Replace tamarind with a teaspoon or two of fresh lime juice.

Tamarind

This large tree, native to tropical Africa, but now found all over India and tropical Asia, produces pods full of reddish, brown pulp that is used to provide a fruity, sour flavor to dishes in many Asian and Latin American cuisines. The pulp from these pods is soaked in water, strained, and added to whatever dish calls for it. You can purchase tamarind in the form of pods; pulp in pressed blocks; or in liquid concentrates to be dissolved in water. Look for tamarind in Latin, Thai, Vietnamese, or Indian markets. If you live in an area where no such markets exist, you can order, as I do, by mail (see page 173).

> All curries do not taste alike; they have as many distinctive bouquets as wine. You can develop into a connoisseur of curries just as you can of other good things of life.—Harvey Day

Curry Leaves

These small, aromatic, dark green leaves are in no way related to curry powder. They come from small trees native to south India and are widely used in the curries of that area and in various preparations all over India. According to Julie Sahni, in *Classic Indian Vegetarian and Grain Cooking*, curry leaves have been grown for use in cooking since ancient times, and were the only flavoring in Vedic Indian cooking. As a result they provided the base of the original, much simpler, curry powder. The first time I tried them in a curry, I found their distinct aroma to be simultaneously very exotic and deeply familiar. Ever since, I have found my taste buds longing for this particular flavor and aroma. You can now find fresh curry leaves in Indian grocery stores. They can be bought through mail order sources and will stay fresh in the refrigerator for up to two weeks.

Pico de Gallo Salsa

$1\frac{1}{2}$ cups

Grocery shelves are stocked full with a huge variety of salsas in jars, but not one of them has the fresh, vibrant flavor of this salsa, which you can put together in minutes. Forget fussy procedures like peeling the tomatoes—all you have to do is chop, chop, chop. Avoid the temptation to use your food processor, which will turn your salsa into soup. You can make Pico de Gallo all year by substituting good-quality canned tomatoes for the fresh, ripe tomatoes of summer.

4 medium-size ripe tomatoes, finely diced
1 small red onion, finely diced
3 jalapeño chilies, cored, seeded, and finely diced
$\frac{1}{4}$ cup finely chopped fresh cilantro
2 teaspoons salt, or more to taste
1 teaspoon sugar
Juice of 1 lime

1. Combine all the ingredients in a bowl and mix well.

2. Serve as a topping for chili, particularly any of the all bean chilies, or as a dip for tortilla chips.

Salsas always put me in the South-of-the-Border mood. Their cool yellows and greens mixed with hot pinks and bright reds make me think of a brilliantly costumed mariachi band. And as for flavors, salsas are like a mini-fiesta for the taste buds: They are at once sharp and sweet, hot and cool.—Mark Miller, *Coyote Cafe*

Other fruits and vegetables provide a meal and pass from memory. Not [chile] peppers. They grab the senses. They make us laugh. They make us cry. They make us think. They make us remember. They connect us to other people. They make us feel human. They make us feel alive.—Susan Hazen-Hammond, *Chile Pepper Fever*

Lentil Curry with Potatoes, Carrots, Spinach, and Chick-peas

4 to 6 servings

The lentils in this curry melt into the background to provide a sauce for the other vegetables. You can reduce the amount of heat in the curry by discarding the seeds and ribs from the chilies, or by adding more chilies to the curry. This recipe is based on one in Didi Emmons's terrific book, Vegetarian Planet.

2 tablespoons canola oil

1 tablespoon butter (optional)

2 large or 3 medium onions, cut in half lengthwise and thinly sliced

6 garlic cloves, finely chopped

2 fresh serrano or jalapeño chilies, finely minced

1 tablespoon finely chopped fresh ginger

2 teaspoons ground coriander

$1\frac{1}{2}$ teaspoons ground cardamom

1 teaspoon ground cumin (see page 172)

1 teaspoon ground turmeric

1 teaspoon paprika

1 teaspoon salt

$\frac{1}{2}$ teaspoon freshly ground black pepper

1 quart water

1 cup red or brown lentils, picked over and rinsed

2 large baking potatoes, peeled and cut into $\frac{1}{2}$-inch cubes

4 carrots, peeled and cut into $\frac{1}{2}$-inch-thick rounds

1 pound fresh spinach, well washed and stems removed, or 1 10-ounce package frozen spinach, thawed

$\frac{1}{2}$ cup cooked chick-peas

2 teaspoons fresh lime juice

1. Heat the oil and butter in a large sauté pan or 3- to 4-quart saucepan over medium heat. Add the onions and sauté, stirring frequently, for 10 to 15 minutes, until

the onions turn golden brown. Add the garlic, chilies, ginger, coriander, cardamom, cumin, turmeric, paprika, salt, and pepper. Sauté for 2 to 3 minutes longer, stirring frequently.

2. Stir in the water and lentils. Bring to a boil, reduce heat to a simmer, and cook for 10 minutes. Add the potatoes and carrots and simmer for 15 to 20 minutes, until the potatoes are tender.

3. Add the spinach and chick-peas and simmer for 5 minutes longer. Taste for seasoning and add salt and pepper, if necessary. Stir in the lime juice and serve with rice.

Cardamom

Cardamom does double duty in the cuisine of India where the whole pods are used to flavor rice and meat dishes, and the ground seeds provide the main flavor in the spice mixture called garam masala. But it is also called "the vanilla of India" because it is used to flavor so many of the traditional dessert preparations. Elsewhere in the world, the pods are used to flavor coffee by the Bedouins, in spice mixtures by the Arabs and Ethiopians, and, in Europe, most especially by the Danes for flavoring in breads and pastries. The seeds can be chewed to sweeten the breath and they also act as a stimulant and digestive. Cardamom pods and ground cardamom are expensive, sometimes hard to find in supermarkets, but available by mail order from Penzey's (see page 173). There is no substitute aromatic spice.

Coriander

If you have ever grown your own cilantro (fresh coriander), and watched in despair as it quickly bolted and went to seed in the summer heat, what you ended up with is coriander seed. These lemon-scented seeds are ground to a powder and make up one of the most widely used seasonings in India. And as the highly aromatic, very pungent fresh coriander leaves are widely used all over the Middle East, India, Asia, and most of the New World, it is possibly the most popular herb in the world. The differences in flavor between the fresh herb and the ground seed are so distinct that many people don't realize that in each case they are dealing with one and the same plant.

Foods having a bitter, acidic, saltish, hot, pungent, and piquant burning taste are liked by those hankering after worldly pleasures, epicureans included.—Bhagavad Gita

Papaya Fruit Curry

A sweet and hot fruit curry provides a welcome change of pace from vegetarian and nonvegetarian cooking. This recipe is very loosely adapted from one I found in Harvey Day's The Complete Book of Curries, *and I have found similar recipes in other books dealing with Indian cooking. This is one of my favorite meals for a winter evening. The short dark days seem to set off a yearning for the sweet rich flavors of fruits and nuts.*

1 papaya, peeled, seeded, and diced

2 cups diced fresh pineapple, or 1 8-oz can pineapple chunks, drained

2 bananas (not too ripe), peeled, sliced lengthwise, and cut into $\frac{1}{2}$-inch chunks

1 large tart apple, peeled, cored, and seeded, cut into $\frac{1}{2}$-inch chunks

Juice of 1 lime or lemon

2 tablespoons unsalted butter or canola oil

2 large onions, cut in half lengthwise and thinly sliced

2 small green chilies (serrano or jalapeño), ribs and seeds removed, finely minced

1 tablespoon Madras curry powder

$\frac{1}{2}$ teaspoon ground ginger

$\frac{1}{4}$ teaspoon cayenne (or more to taste)

$\frac{1}{2}$ teaspoon salt

1 can (14 ounces) low-fat coconut milk

$\frac{1}{4}$ cup raisins

$\frac{1}{2}$ cup dry roasted cashews, coarsely chopped, for garnish

1. Combine the papaya, pineapple, bananas, and apple in a bowl and sprinkle with lime or lemon juice.

2. In a sauté or saucepan, heat the butter or oil over medium heat. Add the onions and cook, stirring frequently, for 10 minutes, until the onions start to turn golden brown. Add the chilies, curry powder, ground ginger, cayenne, and salt. Cook, stirring, for 2 minutes. Add the coconut milk and cook, stirring, for about 5 minutes.

3. Add the fruit and raisins and simmer gently for 20 minutes. Serve in bowls over hot rice and garnish with chopped cashews.

Variations
- You can play around with substituting or adding any number of other fruit. Try seedless grapes, dried apricots, pears, fresh figs.
- You can also play around with adding a vegetable or two to the mix. Try carrots, peas, sweet potatoes, cubed butternut squash, or pumpkin.

Curries have been eaten for centuries. The discovery of vitamins was broadcast to the world by Sir Frederick Gowland Hopkins in 1911. But no one realized that the spices used to make curries are rich in vitamins. . . . The paprika and chilli families are extremely rich in vitamin C, an antiscorbutic vitamin which is good for the skin. This may be one reason why so many Indian women have such remarkably clear skins.—Harvey Day

Curried Mushrooms, Potatoes, and Peas

4 to 6 servings

This is a comforting curry that's very easy to make and easy to eat. As with most other dishes, you can feel free to add or substitute any number of ingredients. When I feel like splurging, I replace some or all of the white mushrooms with fresh, sliced shiitake mushrooms. This recipe is based on one in Charmaine Solomon's encyclopedic book, The Complete Asian Cookbook.

2 tablespoons butter or canola oil

1 medium onion, cut in half lengthwise and finely sliced

4 garlic cloves, finely minced

1 teaspoon grated fresh ginger

2 tablespoons finely chopped fresh cilantro

1 teaspoon ground turmeric

$\frac{1}{2}$ teaspoon cayenne (or to taste)

1 pound small white mushrooms, wiped clean and cut in half

1 pound small red-skinned potatoes, washed, scrubbed, and quartered

1 cup fresh or frozen green peas (if frozen, add peas during last 15 minutes of cooking)

$\frac{1}{2}$ cup water

$1\frac{1}{2}$ teaspoons salt

1 teaspoon garam masala*

1. In a sauté pan or a saucepan, heat the butter or canola oil. Add the onion and cook over medium heat, stirring frequently, for 5 minutes. Add the garlic, ginger, and cilantro and cook, stirring, for 3 minutes longer. Add the turmeric and cayenne and cook, stirring, for another minute.

2. Add the mushrooms, potatoes, and fresh peas along with the water and salt. Stir well, cover, and cook on low heat for 15 minutes. Remove cover, sprinkle with

*You can buy prepared mixtures at Indian markets or by mail order (see page 173).

garam masala, and add frozen peas if that is what you are using. Stir well, cover and cook for an additional 15 minutes, until the potatoes are completely tender. Serve with rice.

The aim of the curry eater is not to bolt his food, but to savor it. Flavour then, is all important. This enjoyment of food has a stronger psychological bearing on health than we realize.

First, there is the anticipation, caused by the appetizing aroma of curry. Digestive juices are secreted in the mouth. Then follows the real pleasures of eating with enjoyment. Contentment, naturally, is the result, and in its train, sound health.—Harvey Day

The Basics

Light Vegetable Stock

2 quarts

10 cups water

1 cup chopped fresh spinach

2 unpeeled onions, quartered

1 leek, trimmed, rinsed, and sliced

3 carrots, scrubbed but not peeled, coarsely chopped

3 parsnips, scrubbed but not peeled, coarsely chopped

3 small inner celery ribs, including leaves, coarsely chopped

1 bunch fresh parsley, including stems, coarsely chopped

2 bay leaves

4 garlic cloves, smashed with a knife

6 whole coriander seeds

6 whole black peppercorns

1 small dried hot chili pepper (optional)

Combine all the ingredients in a soup pot and bring to a boil. Immediately reduce heat to a simmer and simmer over low heat for 40 minutes. Strain the broth and discard all the vegetables. The broth can be refrigerated for up to 5 days or frozen for a longer time.

Rich, Full-Flavored Vegetable Broth

There are times when I want a vegetable broth that is rich, full of flavor, and even has some body to it. I have found that by using a lot (sometimes 2 or 3 heads) of garlic and adding potato peels, kombu seaweed, and some heat from cayenne, I get exactly what I'm looking for.

This vegetable broth will keep for several days in the refrigerator, but should be frozen if you want to keep it around for any longer than that. It will keep in the freezer for several months.

2 tablespoons flavorful olive oil

1 large onion, coarsely chopped

2 large carrots, coarsely chopped

2 celery ribs, some leaves included, coarsely chopped

12 to 18 garlic cloves, unpeeled and smashed

2 leeks, white and pale green parts only, thinly sliced

$\frac{1}{2}$ pound sliced mushrooms

2 2-inch pieces of kombu seaweed (optional)

Peel from 2 large baking potatoes (optional)

$\frac{1}{2}$ cup finely chopped parsley, including the stems

$\frac{1}{4}$ cup chopped fresh basil

2 bay leaves

1 teaspoon dried marjoram

3 sprigs fresh thyme, or $\frac{1}{2}$ teaspoon dried thyme

1 teaspoon salt, or to taste

10 whole black peppercorns

$\frac{1}{4}$ teaspoon cayenne

1. Heat the olive oil in a large heavy saucepan over medium heat and sauté the onion, carrots, and celery until they start to color, 10 to 15 minutes.

2. Stir in the garlic, leeks, and mushrooms and cook, stirring, for 5 minutes longer.

3. Add 3 quarts water, the optional kombu seaweed and potato peels, parsley, basil, bay leaves, marjoram, thyme, salt, peppercorns, and cayenne. Bring to a boil, reduce heat to low, and simmer, partially covered, for a minimum of 30 minutes and preferably for as long as 2 hours.

4. Strain the stock through a sieve, pressing the solids down with a wooden spoon to extract all the liquid. Taste for seasoning and add salt, pepper, and cayenne to taste.

Variation

All sorts of ingredients from your vegetable bin can make their way into a vegetable stock. Consider turnips, parsnips, zucchini, shredded salad greens, spinach, fennel. I leave out vegetables with very strong flavors such as cabbage, broccoli, beets, bell peppers, asparagus.

Risotto Vegetable Broth

In just one hour you can have a light vegetable stock ready to use for risotto. You can leave out the leek or substitute some scallions. If you don't have fresh thyme, replace it with ¼ teaspoon dried thyme.

2 quarts cold water

3 medium onions, quartered

3 carrots, scrubbed and cut into large chunks

2 celery ribs, scrubbed and cut into large chunks

1 small leek, thoroughly cleaned, some of green part included, cut into large
  chunks

2 bay leaves

1 garlic clove, smashed

Small handful of parsley with stems

Several fresh thyme sprigs

1 teaspoon salt

1. Combine all the ingredients in a soup pot and bring to a simmer over medium heat. Cook, uncovered, at a bare simmer for 50 to 60 minutes.

2. Strain the broth, discarding all the vegetables and herbs. Use the broth right away or refrigerate for a couple of days.

Basic White Rice

This method applies to all varieties of long-grain rice, including basmati and jasmine.

When cooking rice, remember that the larger amount of water will yield a soft, very moist rice, while the lesser amount will yield firmer, more separate grains.

1 cup long-grain rice
1¾ to 2 cups water
½ to 1 teaspoon salt
1 tablespoon unsalted butter (optional)

1. Place the rice, water, salt, and butter in a heavy 1-quart saucepan. Bring to a boil over high heat. Stir once, reduce the heat to low, cover, and cook for 15 to 20 minutes, until the water has been absorbed.

2. Remove from heat and let stand, covered, for 10 minutes. Fluff rice with a fork and serve. Any leftover rice can be refrigerated for several days or frozen in airtight containers for several months. Reheat in a double boiler or microwave.

Basmati or Jasmine Rice

Both basmati and jasmine rice are types of aromatic rice that have pronounced, very pleasing aromas. Basmati, originally from India and Pakistan, is now grown also in the United States, as is jasmine rice, originally from Thailand.

Basic Brown Rice

I like the chewy, moist texture of short-grain brown rice, but the long-grain brown rice will work just as well in this recipe. If you find that you don't have time for the preliminary soaking, simply add an extra cup of water to the rice and 15 minutes additional cooking time.

2 cups short-grain brown rice
4 cups boiling water
1 teaspoon salt (or more to taste)

1. Wash the brown rice in several changes of cold water and soak it in cold water for 1 hour.

2. Drain the rice and pour into a heavy casserole or Dutch oven. Cook the rice, stirring with a wooden spoon, over medium-high heat until all the water evaporates and the rice starts to toast and is starting to brown slightly.

3. Add the water and salt, turn the heat to low, stir well, cover, and cook over low heat for 1 hour, or until the water has been absorbed and the rice is tender. Turn off the heat and let stand in covered pot for 10 to 15 minutes before serving.

Note

Cooked rice can be refrigerated in a plastic container for a week or frozen for as long as 6 weeks. It reheats perfectly in a microwave oven, or in a nonstick pan with a few tablespoons of water.

Steamed Wild Rice

$3\frac{1}{2}$ to 4 cups

1 cup wild rice
3 cups water
1 teaspoon salt

Put the rice in a large bowl of cold water and scrub the grains between the palms of your hands. Drain the rice in a strainer. Bring the water and salt to a boil. Add the wild rice, reduce heat, and simmer, partially covered, until tender. This will take anywhere from 40 to 60 minutes. Remove from heat and let the rice stand, covered, for 10 minutes to absorb any remaining liquid. Transfer the rice to a large salad bowl.

Basic Pearl Barley

about $3\frac{1}{2}$ cups

3 cups water
$\frac{1}{2}$ teaspoon salt
1 tablespoon unsalted butter or canola oil (optional)
1 cup pearl barley, rinsed

1. In a medium-sized saucepan, bring the water, salt and butter or canola oil to a boil. Stir in the barley, lower the heat to a simmer, cover the saucepan and simmer gently for 45 minutes.

2. Remove from heat and let stand covered for 15 minutes before serving.

Basic Couscous

about $3\frac{1}{2}$ cups

 You can use either regular or whole wheat couscous in this recipe. Either way the grains are ready to eat in about 12 minutes.

$1\frac{1}{2}$ cups vegetable broth or water

1 tablespoon extra-virgin olive oil

$\frac{1}{2}$ teaspoon salt

1 cup couscous

1. In a medium-size saucepan, bring the broth or water, olive oil, and salt to a boil. Add the couscous, lower the heat slightly, and cook, stirring frequently, for 1 minute.

2. Remove saucepan from heat, cover, and let stand for 10 minutes, or until the couscous has absorbed all the liquid. Fluff the couscous with a fork and serve.

Basic Quinoa

$3\frac{1}{2}$ to 4 cups

Quinoa, pronounced KEEN-wah, may be a new grain for us, but its use goes back to the Inca civilization. The Incas referred to the tiny, oval seeds as their sacred mother grains. And nutritionally, it is in all ways a superior grain, extremely high in protein, also niacin, iron, phosphorous, and potassium.

1 cup quinoa

2 cups vegetable broth or water

$\frac{1}{2}$ teaspoon salt, or to taste

OPTIONAL SEASONINGS

1 garlic clove, finely minced

1 shallot, finely minced

$\frac{1}{4}$ teaspoon or more freshly ground black pepper

1. Place the quinoa in a deep bowl, cover with plenty of cold water, and rub the quinoa between the palms of your hands for 5 to 10 seconds. Drain the quinoa in a strainer and repeat the process.

2. Bring the stock or water to a boil in a 1-quart saucepan, add the quinoa, salt, and any of the optional seasonings. Lower heat to a simmer, cover the pan, and cook for 15 minutes, until all the liquid is absorbed. Remove from heat and let stand, still covered, for 5 minutes. Fluff with a fork and serve, or let cool for use in a salad.

Polenta

6 to 8 servings

The most basic polenta is nothing but water, salt, and cornmeal. If you want to make that, simply omit the other ingredients. But the simple addition of butter and garlic to the cooking water transforms an ordinary dish into something quite tasty and extraordinary. As for the method of making polenta, there are various approaches. Some cooks like to make a paste with the cornmeal and cold water before stirring into the hot water, while others insist on the classical method of stirring a fine stream of cornmeal into violently boiling water. The method described below is easy, quick, and lump-free.

7 cups water
1 teaspoon salt
3 tablespoons unsalted butter
3 garlic cloves, crushed
2 cups coarsely ground cornmeal

1. Bring the water to a boil in a large heavy pot. (The water should not come more than halfway up the sides of the pot.) Turn off the heat. Stir in salt, butter, and garlic. Then stir in cornmeal, pouring it in a fine, steady stream as you stir.

2. Place the pot over medium-high heat and continue stirring as the cornmeal boils and thickens. Make sure to use a long-handled wooden spoon and to stand back from the pot so the bubbles don't explode in your face. As the cornmeal thickens, the boiling mass might get violent. Simply turn off the heat and keep stirring. When it has

calmed down, turn up the heat and continue cooking until done. The total cooking time is 15 to 20 minutes. The polenta is done when it forms a very thick mass and starts to pull away from the sides of the pot as you stir. Serve hot.

Variations

Fried or grilled polenta is good when you want to make part of the meal ahead. It is also a good way to serve polenta to a large crowd.

Fried Polenta: Make polenta as described in previous recipe, then pour either into an oiled 9 x 5 x 3-inch loaf pan or 9 x 12-inch roasting pan and cover with plastic wrap and refrigerate for several hours or overnight. (The dimensions of both the loaf pan and the roasting pan are not critical; use any pans you have that are about that size.) Cut polenta into $\frac{1}{2}$-inch slices or into squares, triangles, or even circles, using a cookie cutter. Heat about 2 tablespoons olive oil or olive oil mixed with butter in a large skillet and fry the polenta pieces until golden brown on both sides.

Grilled Polenta: Prepare polenta as for fried polenta. Brush polenta pieces with olive oil on each side and grill over hot coals or under a broiler for about 2 minutes on each side, until golden brown.

Fried mush came along in the fall, after the first harvest of winter corn and before the pancake season set in, and again in the spring when the batter pitcher was washed and put away. Fried mush for breakfast followed a preceding supper of mush and milk. My mother made her mush by sifting yellow corn meal, fresh from the mill, into an iron kettle of boiling salted water; with one hand she sifted the meal while with the other she stirred it with a wooden spoon. It was then drawn to the back of the stove to bubble and sputter and spurt for an hour or longer—and woe to you if it happened to spurt onto bare hand or arm while stirring.

Whatever mush was left over after supper was packed into a greased bread tin. In the morning this was sliced and fried in hot fat, and eaten with butter and syrup.—Della T. Lutes, *The Country Kitchen*

Roasted Acorn Squash

The quantity in this recipe depends on how many people you are serving. Select one acorn squash for every two people. I always like to make a few extra, for people who want seconds or for leftovers the next day.

acorn squash, 1 for every 2 people
melted butter
salt
brown sugar
orange juice

1. Preheat the oven to 400°F.

2. Cut acorn squash in half, either across the midsection or lengthwise. Scoop out the seeds and stringy parts. Brush the cut surfaces with melted butter and sprinkle with salt.

3. Arrange the squash in a baking pan, cut side down, and film the bottom of the pan with $\frac{1}{4}$-inch of water. Bake for 30 minutes.

4. Turn the squash over, brush insides with melted butter, and sprinkle with brown sugar. Bake for 15 to 30 minutes longer, until tender, basting occasionally with a tablespoon or two of orange juice.

Balsamic Vinaigrette

$\frac{3}{4}$ cup

Try to use the best quality balsamic vinegar you can afford. If your vinegar is thin and very acid, cut the amount by half. The higher the quality of the balsamic vinegar, the less oil you can use.

1 teaspoon coarse salt
1 garlic clove, peeled

4 tablespoons balsamic vinegar

2 teaspoons red wine vinegar

5 tablespoons extra-virgin olive oil

1. In a mortar, pound the salt and garlic to a paste.

2. Whisk in the vinegars until the salt has dissolved. Whisk in the olive. Taste the vinaigrette and adjust vinegar and olive oil to your taste. If the vinegar taste is too strong and you don't want to add more olive oil, whisk in 1 teaspoon water at a time, up to 3 teaspoons.

Variation
Substitute raspberry or other fruit vinegar for the balsamic vinegar.

Harissa

1 cup

Harissa, a paste made from chilies and seasonings, is a spicy condiment found all over the Middle East. Serve with grains like couscous and all manner of stews.

1 ounce (about 1 cup) dried red chilies

1 garlic clove, peeled

1 teaspoon salt

2 teaspoons fresh lemon juice

Extra-virgin olive oil

1. Put the chilies in a small saucepan with just enough water to cover. Bring to a simmer and remove from heat. Let stand for 45 minutes to 1 hour. Drain the chilies.

2. Place the chilies and the garlic in the bowl of a food processor or electric blender. Add the salt and 1 teaspoon fresh lemon juice. Purée the chilies to a paste, adding more lemon juice to the mixture if it seems dry.

3. Transfer the mixture to a small bowl or jar and add enough olive oil to film the top. Serve at once or store, covered, in the refrigerator for up to 2 weeks.

Black Beans

1 pound (2 cups) dried black beans
2 tablespoons olive oil
1 large onion, diced
3 garlic cloves, minced
2 tablespoons toasted, ground cumin
1 tablespoon salt, or to taste

1. Pick over the beans to remove any foreign objects. Wash the beans and soak them in water for at least 6 hours or overnight, changing the water several times.

2. Heat the oil in a large heavy pot over low heat. Add the onion and garlic and cook, stirring, for 5 minutes, until the onion has wilted.

3. Drain the beans and add them to the onion and garlic, along with enough water to cover by 2 inches. Add the cumin and bring to a boil. Reduce heat to low and simmer, uncovered, for 3 hours or longer, until the beans are very tender. Stir the beans from time to time and make sure that there is enough liquid to cover the beans. Add salt during the last half hour of cooking.

Gomasio

Gomasio is a wonderful Japanese seasoning salt with the rich, full flavor of toasted sesame seeds. Use it instead of table salt to enhance steamed vegetables, salads, or any other food to which you might want to add salt. A jar of gomasio makes an original and welcome hostess gift.

1 cup unhulled sesame seeds
4 teaspoons sea salt or kosher salt, or to taste

1. Rinse the seeds in several changes of cold water and drain well.

2. Place a heavy cast-iron skillet over medium-high heat and put in the sesame seeds. Roast the seeds, stirring constantly, for 8 to 12 minutes, until they have started to color and give off a pleasant, toasted aroma. Add the salt for the last minute of roasting.

3. Transfer the sesame seeds and salt to a food processor and pulse on and off a few times to a coarse ground consistency. Taste and add more salt, if you wish. Cool completely and store in the refrigerator in a tightly covered jar.

Roasting and Peeling
Fresh Chilies

Fresh chilies are often roasted and peeled before using them in sauces or on their own. This concentrates the sugars in the flesh, giving the chilies a more intense, slightly smoky flavor. Another reason for roasting the chilies is to be able to remove the skin, which often has an unpleasant bitter flavor. The exceptions are jalapeños and serranos, which are usually finely diced, skin and all.

Chilies can be roasted over a hot charcoal grill, or on a wire rack over an open flame on top of the stove.

1. Cut a small slit in the chili close to the stem to allow steam to escape.

2. Blister the chilies over hot coals or over the open flame on top of your stove. Turn the chilies frequently so they can blister evenly all over. The chilies may burn slightly, but do not let them turn completely black.

3. Wrap the chilies in damp paper towels and place in a plastic bag to let them steam for 15 minutes, or until they have cooled.

4. Split each chili open with a knife and peel away as much of the blistered skin as possible.

The chilies are now ready to use or freeze. Do not keep roasted chilies for longer than a day or two in the refrigerator as they spoil very quickly.

If you know you are planning to freeze the chilies, roast them but do not peel them. Let them cool and freeze them. They will be much easier to peel when they have thawed.

Roasted Garlic

Garlic becomes a totally new ingredient once it has been slowly roasted together with olive oil. It has a nutty, mellow sweetness along with a soft, spreadable texture. In this guise it has so many uses that you may want to keep some always on hand. Use roasted garlic as a spread for bread or crackers, add it to sauces and gravies to thicken and add flavor. Use it in salad dressings and pasta sauces. Just be sure to choose heads that are unblemished and where the cloves are tightly grown together. Don't use garlic that has brown or soft spots or garlic that is starting to sprout.

2 to 4 whole heads of garlic, or 1 cup garlic cloves, unpeeled
$\frac{1}{4}$ cup extra-virgin olive oil
$\frac{1}{4}$ cup water

1. Preheat the oven to 350°F.

2. If you are roasting whole heads of garlic, loosen the papery outside skin by rolling the heads around on a hard surface. Discard any loosened skin. Use a sharp knife to cut away about $\frac{1}{2}$ inch from the top end of the garlic head so that the insides of most of the cloves are visible. If you are using garlic cloves, loosen their skins by pressing down on the cloves with the flat side of a chef's knife. Press the knife with the heel of your hand until you feel a slight yielding to the pressure.

3. In a small casserole, combine the garlic, oil, and water. Toss well to make sure the garlic is coated with oil. Cover the casserole tightly with foil.

4. Bake for 45 minutes, then check to see if the garlic is completely soft inside by squeezing a clove until it opens and a garlic purée oozes out. If the garlic is still solid, or you are roasting whole heads of garlic, continue to bake, uncovered, for 30 minutes longer.

5. Remove from oven and let garlic cool in the casserole. If you are not using the garlic right away, wrap each head of garlic in foil and refrigerate until needed. Store the separate cloves in a jar together with the oil, or peel the cloves and purée them together with the oil. Roasted garlic will keep in the refrigerator for 2 to 3 weeks.

Toasted, Ground Cumin Seeds

Toasting cumin seeds brings out their flavor to great advantage and removes any trace of a raw taste that many people find objectionable.

1. Place a small heavy skillet over medium heat. Place 4 tablespoons of cumin seeds in the skillet and cook, stirring, for about 3 minutes, until the seeds start to turn color and emit a delicious, roasted aroma.

2. Remove the seeds to a dish or paper towel and let them cool slightly. Place them in the container of a spice grinder (a clean coffee grinder will do) and grind them to a powder. Store in a small jar with a tight-fitting lid.

Mail-order Sources

Adriana's Caravan
409 Vanderbilt Street
Brooklyn, NY 11218
Phone: 800-316-0820 or 718-436-8565
Spices and herbs. Chilies, mushrooms, and specialty foods from around the world. Here you can find blocks of tamarind, fish sauce, lemongrass, and curry leaves.

Elizabeth Berry
Gallina Canyon Ranch
Box 706
Abiqui, NM 87510
Send $1.00 and a self-addressed stamped envelope for catalog. Incredible selection of heirloom beans.

Gold Mine Natural Foods
3419 Hancock Street
San Diego, CA 92102
Phone: 800-475-FOOD
Organic everything. Grains, beans, lentils, flours, whole dried chestnuts, tamari, etc.

Penzey's, Ltd.
P.O. Box 933
Muskego, WI 53150
Phone: 414-679-7207
Fax: 414-679-7878
A huge selection of spices, herbs, and seasonings. All very fresh at very good prices. Call for free catalog.

Bibliography

Barrett, Judith, and Norma Wasserman. *Risotto.* New York: Collier Books. Macmillan Publishing Company, 1987

Bertolli, Paul, with Alice Waters. *Chez Panisse Cooking.* New York: Random House, 1988

Capon, Robert Farrar. *The Supper of the Lamb.* New York: Doubleday & Co., Inc., 1967

Child, Julia. *In Julia Child's Kitchen.* New York: Alfred A. Knopf, 1996

Collin, Rima & Richard. *The New Orleans Cookbook,* New York: Alfred A. Knopf, 1975

Cost, Bruce. *Bruce Cost's Asian Ingredients.* New York: William Morrow and Company, Inc., 1988

Day, Harvey. *The Complete Book of Curries.* London: Kaye & Ward, 1970

DeWitt, Dave, and Arthur Pais. *A World of Curries.* Boston: Little, Brown and Company, 1994

DeWitt, Dave, Mary Jane Wilan, and Melissa T. Stock. *Hot and Spicy and Meatless.* Rocklin, CA: Prima Publishing, 1994

Emmons, Didi. *Vegetarian Planet.* Boston: The Harvard Common Press, 1997

Grigson, Jane. *Jane Grigson's Vegetable Book.* New York: Atheneum, 1979

Grunes, Barbara, and Virginia Van Vynck. *All-American Waves of Grain.* New York: Henry Holt and Company, 1997

Hom, Ken. *Asian Vegetarian Feast.* New York: William Morrow and Company, Inc., 1988

Jaffrey, Madhur. *World-of-the-East Vegetarian Cooking.* New York: Alfred A. Knopf, 1983

London, Sheryl and Mel. *Sheryl and Mel London's Creative Cooking with Grains and Pasta.* Emmaus, PA: Rodale Press, 1982

Luongo, Pino. *A Tuscan in the Kitchen.* New York: Clarkson N. Potter, Inc., 1988

Madison, Deborah. *Vegetarian Cooking for Everyone.* New York: Broadway Books, 1997

Madison, Deborah, with Edward Espe Brown. *The Greens Cook Book.* New York: Bantam Books, Inc., 1987

McDermott, Nancie. *Real Vegetarian Thai.* San Francisco: Chronicle Books, 1997

Robbins, Maria. *Chili!.* New York: St. Martin's Griffin, 1995

———. *American Corn*. New York: St. Martin's Press, 1989

———. *A Cook's Alphabet of Quotations*. Hopewell, NJ: The Ecco Press, 1997

Romer, Elizabeth. *The Tuscan Year*. New York: Atheneum, 1985

Root, Waverley. *Food. An Authoritative and Visual History and Dictionary of the Foods of the World*. New York: Simon and Schuster, 1980

Rozin, Elizabeth. *Blue Corn and Chocolate*. New York: Alfred A. Knopf, 1992

Sahni, Julie. *Classic Indian Vegetarian and Grain Cooking*. New York: William Morrow and Company, Inc., 1985

Sass, Lorna J. *Great Vegetarian Cooking Under Pressure*. New York: William Morrow and Company, Inc., 1994

———. *Recipes From an Ecological Kitchen*. New York: William Morrow and Company, Inc., 1992

Simmons, Marie. *Rice, The Amazing Grain*. New York: Henry Holt and Company, Inc., 1991

Solomon, Charmaine. *The Complete Asian Cookbook*. New York: McGraw-Hill Book Company, 1985

Thompson, Jennifer Trainer. *Jump Up and Kiss Me*. Berkeley, CA: Ten Speed Press, 1996

Thorne, John. *Simple Cooking*. New York: Viking Penguin, Inc., 1987

Waldron, Maggie. *Cold Spaghetti at Midnight*. New York: William Morrow and Company, Inc., 1992

Waters, Alice. *Chez Panisse Vegetables*. New York: HarperCollins Publishers, Inc., 1996

Wells, Patricia. *Trattoria*. New York: William Morrow and Company, Inc., 1993

Wood, Rebecca. *The Splendid Grain*. New York: William Morrow and Company, Inc., 1997

Yin-Fei Lo, Eileen. *From the Earth: Chinese Vegetarian Cooking*. New York: Macmillan, Inc., 1995

MAGAZINES

Thorne, John, and Matt Lewis. "Desperately Resisting Risotto," *Simple Cooking*, Autumn 1995 Issue No. 44

Index